Japanese

Japanese

Hideo Dekura

Published in 2014 by
New Holland Publishers
London • Sydney • Cape Town • Auckland

The Chandlery Unit 114 50 Westminster Bridge Road London SE1 7QY UK
1/66 Gibbes Street Chatswood NSW 2067 Australia
Wembley Square First Floor Solan Road Gardens Cape Town 8001 South Africa
218 Lake Road Northcote Auckland New Zealand

www.newhollandpublishers.com

ISBN: 9781742575339

Managing Director: Fiona Schultz
Publisher: Fiona Schultz
Designer: Lorena Susak
Project Editor: Emily Carryer
Production Director: Olga Dementiev
Printer: Toppan Leefung Printing Ltd (China)

10 9 8 7 6 5 4 3 2 1

Follow New Holland Publishers on
Facebook: www.facebook.com/NewHollandPublishers

Contents

Introduction

The History of Japanese Food

The close relationship between the Japanese people and rice has been a feature of Japanese culture over the passage of time. Introduced from China and Korea at the beginning of Japanese history more than 2000 years ago, rice soon became such an important part of Japanese life that many ceremonies are associated with its growth cycle.

Japanese cuisine had its earliest roots in the beliefs of *Shintoism*, which greatly influenced the styles and motifs used in food, which was often part of the offering ceremonies to the Shinto gods. Korean and Chinese styles of vegetarian cuisine were then introduced, along with Buddhism, around the 8th century, and these were readily absorbed into Japanese culture and beliefs.

During the Heian era (794–1185 AD), Japanese culture continued to flourish and absorb ideas from other Asian continents. Food preparation and cooking techniques were developed further in this period, including more sophisticated methods of steaming, stewing, pickling and grilling. Using these techniques, the Japanese people created the distinctive manner and fundamental styles of Japanese food that we know today, such as soup, stocks, pickles, sushi and sashimi. The *Zen* philosophy of Buddhism exerted a great influence on Japanese culture, teaching the theory of 'wabi' (quiet refinement) and 'sabi' (elegant simplicity); concepts which are still being developed in Japanese cuisine. The *Zen* influence is apparent in what is considered the proper way to handle ingredients, present Japanese dishes, and entertain guests.

Formal, ceremonial meals developed soon after the conclusion of the civil war era (1192–1333 AD). *Honzen-ryori*, one of the most formal full-course Japanese meals, introduced the practice of serving one soup and three dishes on a miniature table, using gorgeous lacquerware and crockery. (The miniature table has evolved into a tray at many restaurants today.) This led to the development of *chakaiseki-ryori* (*kaiseki*), a full course meal and tea ceremony, and *kaiseki-ryori*, a full course banquet.

The first official cooking groups and schools were founded around 1300 AD. These schools have upheld traditions and passed them down through many generations. Through these schools Japanese culinary skills have been maintained in all their beauty and tradition for more than 700 years.

In the Edo era (1600–1867 AD) the government cut off their relationships with other countries and a national isolation policy was enacted. Under these circumstances, Japanese culture found its own way, producing developments in the tea ceremony, food culture, and most of the Japanese arts without influences from any other countries. When the isolation policy ended, the people were so excited to meet the unknown western culture that the society underwent a remarkable change in its culture and traditions. Many foods were introduced from Europe, such as bread, coffee, confectioneries, whisky, and wine. Moreover, the habit of eating meat became widely accepted among the people of Japan.

However, the last decade has seen a striking revival of Japanese traditions, including food culture, in Japan. The number of restaurants and food industries in Japan reached a peak just before the year 2000. Throughout the history of Japanese food, changes in society and influences from overseas have had marked effects. Without these, Japanese food could not have developed into the wonderful cuisine that we know today.

Japanese Food Today

In every culture, eating and drinking together play a significant role in creating and maintaining relationships. Japanese meals vary according to the needs of the occasion. The main styles are the family meal, the packed meal and the formal meal. There are four fundamental types of traditional full-course Japanese formal meals today: *honzen-ryori*, an assembly of dishes served on a tray at formal banquets; *chakaiseki-ryori*, a series of dishes served before the tea ceremony; *kaiseki-ryori*, a series of dishes for parties, often served at restaurants specialising in Japanese cuisine (*ryotei*); and *shojin-ryori*, Buddhist vegetarian dishes.

The art of Japanese food arrangement is characterised by certain broad concepts. Foremost among these is the concept that empty space has a beauty of its own. The balance between vessel and space, and space and food, are also considered crucial. This balance varies according to the season, the design of the utensils and tableware, the type of food, the venue, and even the age of the guests. When multicoloured foods are arranged on serving dishes, great attention is paid to spacing—where and how to leave empty areas to best emphasise the beauty of the dish. This is based on the concept of *ma*: space as a dynamic entity, and an integral and vital component of any composition. The beauty of a finished dish is considered as important as the various ingredients that go into its composition.

Traditionally, the Japanese take their meals seated on *tatami* floor matting, with a small tray-table for each diner. This is still common at traditional Japanese restaurants or inn-style hotels. In Japan, individual servings are laid out on each tray-table beforehand, and carried to the diners. Timing is essential: one must be alert to the guests' state of mind and offer the meal at the proper juncture. The menu may be written in one of three styles of calligraphy: *shin, gyo* and *so. Shin* (plain, true) is a clear, basic style; *gyo* (running) is a more cursive style; and *so* (grass) is a still more cursive form. The style of the calligraphy on the menu is a clear indication of the style of food presentation the diner can expect of that dish.

The Japanese have an overwhelming predilection for odd numbers, based on the ancient philosophy of yin and yang and the five elements. According to this philosophy, even numbers are *yin* (negative), and odd ones are *yang* (positive). This belief is reflected in Japanese cooking to this day; witness *sashimi*, which is usually presented in groups of three, five or seven slices.

It is impossible to discuss Japanese culture without reference to nature. Japan's climate is characterised by pronounced seasonal changes, and the rhythms of life inevitably follow the shifting seasons. The Japanese are very observant of the changes of season, and prepare dishes to reflect these changes. This sensitivity to the seasons is at its strongest in the tea ceremony. In *kaiseki-ryori*, select foods are served on individual trays as part of the tea ceremony, with a special emphasis placed on the three *ki*: *kisetsu* (season), *ki* (vessel) and *kikai* (occasion). Each occasion is considered unique, and hospitality is heightened by serving fresh food, in season, to bring out the flavour, aroma and colour of the ingredients.

According to an old proverb, eating the first produce of the season adds seventy-five days to one's life, so Japanese people always look forward to welcoming a new season. Four seasonal recipes are featured on the following pages, each celebrating the bounty one of the seasons.

Spring

GRILLED SNAPPER COVERED WITH SALT

serves 4

You will need 2 steel BBQ skewers for each snapper

4 whole small snapper, 300 g (10 oz) each
1 tablespoon mirin
½ cup (125 g/4 oz) ground rock salt
4 lemon wedges
soy sauce
8 red radishes, thinly sliced

Spring is the season in which every creature starts to wake up after winter. The wealth of marine and farm products in this season is a delight, and a plate of sushi can reflect the sudden joy of nature blossoming in the garden. Pink cherry blossom is the most loved spring flower in Japan, and this colour often extends to spring dishes. Here it is seen in the colour of the baby snapper and radishes.

Preheat the oven to 180°C (350°F).

Scale the snappers and make a shallow slit along the belly side of each fish. Remove and discard the insides, washing well under running water. Wipe dry thoroughly with paper towels. Place a fish on its side on a cutting board. Push a skewer all the way through the tail just above the line of the backbone. Without removing the skewer, push it back through the fish at a point near the top edge of the fish, level with the gills. The skewer should run along the outside of the fish, thus creating a slight curve through its body. Push another skewer through the tail just below the line of the backbone. Without removing the skewer, push it back through the fish at a point near the belly edge of the fish, just behind the gills. Repeat for each fish. Sprinkle over the mirin and rock salt.

Place the fish on a lightly oiled baking tray in the middle of the oven. Cook for 10 minutes with the door kept open to ensure good air circulation. This will give the flesh a slightly drier texture and a more intense flavour. Preheat the grill to medium heat. Transfer to the grill and cook until the skin becomes a nice brown colour. Test to see if the fish is cooked through by inserting a bamboo skewer near the bone. If juice appears on the surface, keep cooking.

To serve, remove the skewers, arrange the fish on serving plates and garnish each with a lemon wedge. Arrange sliced red radish over one side of each fish. Offer soy sauce on the side for dipping.

SPRING SUSHI
This recipe is pictured together with pieces of Kakumaki (Square Nori Roll) sushi.

Spring: Grilled snapper covered with salt and served with Kakumaki

Summer: Green tea soba
and somen noodles

Summer

GREEN TEA SOBA AND SOMEN NOODLES

serves 4

4 litres (8 pints) water
120 g (4 oz) somen, divided into four equal bunches
120 g (4 oz) green tea soba, divided into four equal bunches ice cubes
12 pieces canned mandarine
2 spring onion (scallions) stems, chopped, or 4 Japanese basil flowers
shichimi (Japanese seven-spice powder) and wasabi to serve

DIPPING SAUCE
½ cup (125 ml/4 fl oz) Bonito Dashi
½ cup (125 ml/4 fl oz) soy sauce
½ cup (125 ml/4 fl oz) mirin

Cold drinks and light dishes are appropriate for a hot summer's day. A bowl of chilled noodles, sashimi on a bed of ice, and fresh salads are cooling and provide stamina.

Bring 2 litres (4 pints) of water to the boil in a large saucepan. Tie one end of each bunch of somen with a rubber band. Put the somen in the boiling water and cook for 2–3 minutes until al dente. Drain, then rinse the somen thoroughly under running water to remove the starch. Drain well again.

Bring another 2 litres (4 pints) of water to the boil. Divide the soba into 2 bundles, and tie one end of each with a rubber band. Put the soba in the boiling water and cook until al dente, or according to the directions on the packet. Drain, then rinse the soba thoroughly. Drain well again.

Place the ice cubes in 4 deep serving bowls. Place 2 bamboo sticks across the top of each bowl. Cut off the tied ends of the somen and soba and hang the noodles on the

bamboo sticks. Arrange the mandarines on the ice.

To make the dipping sauce, combine all the ingredients in a bowl. Divide the sauce among the 4 serving bowls. Place the spring onion or basil flowers, shichimi and wasabi on a plate where diners can help themselves.

To eat, place the spring onions, shichimi and wasabi in the dipping sauce. Dip the noodles into the sauce before eating.

Autumn

Fuki-yose of autumn vegetables

serves **4**

4 chestnuts

8 ginkgo nuts

1 cup (250 g/80 oz) rock salt

2 tablespoons olive oil

8 shimeji mushrooms

8 nameko mushrooms (enoki may be
  substituted if nameko are not available)

4 fresh shitake mushrooms

12 momiji (maple-leaf) shaped carrots

2 tablespoons sake (Japanese rice wine)

8 dried yuzu pieces

80 g (2¾ oz) daikon, grated

4 chives, finely chopped

SAUCE

¼ cup (60 ml/2 fl oz) Bonito Dashi
  (see page 144)

¼ cup (60 ml/2 fl oz) soy sauce

¼ cup (60 ml/2 fl oz) mirin

The vegetables in this dish are cooked on heated stones. You will need about 2 cups of medium-sized stones and some wire mesh to place them on for cooking. A cake-cooling rack may suffice. Yuzu-miso can be used in place of the sauce.

Preheat the oven to 180°C (350°F).

To prepare the chestnuts and ginkgo nuts, make a tiny slit in each shell. Place the chestnuts and ginkgo nuts in 2 separate pots of water and bring the water to the boil in both. The ginkgo nuts will need 10 minutes over medium heat and the chestnuts 15 minutes. Drain the nuts when they are done.

Place a wire mesh over an element on the stove top, add the stones and heat. Alternatively, place the stones beneath an oven grill. The stones are hot enough when a few drops of water placed on them fizz and evaporate instantly. Spread the rock salt in a medium-sized gratin dish or a clay cooking pot, and place the dish in the oven for 10 minutes.

Take the dish out of the oven, and place it on a pot stand. With tongs, place the heated stones on the dish. Sprinkle with olive oil. Arrange the chestnuts, nuts, shimeji, nameko and shitake mushrooms and carrots on the stones, and sprinkle with sake. Cover with aluminium foil or a lid, and set aside outside the oven for about 15 minutes to steam.

To make the sauce, combine the dashi, soy sauce and mirin in a pan. Simmer gently for 5 minutes. Pour the sauce into 4 dipping bowls and divide the yuzu among the bowls.

Transfer the dish with the vegetables to the table and remove the foil or lid. Serve with grated daikon, chopped chives, and sauce on the side.

Autumn: Fuki-yose of
autumn vegetables

Winter: Beef mizutaki
hot pot

Winter

Beef mizutaki hot pot

serves 4

4 dried shitake mushrooms

80 g (2¾ oz) harusame (Japanese
  vermicelli)

100 g (3½ oz) momen-dofu
  (firm beancurd), quartered

40 g (1½ oz) takenoko (bamboo shoots),
  diced

4 strips kombu (kelp), each
  1cm (⅜ in)x 4cm (1½ in), knotted

400 g (14 oz) beef, thinly sliced

8 shungiku (spring chrysanthemum) leaves

12 shimeji mushrooms

6 cups (1.5 litres/3 pints) Bonito Dashi

DIPPING SAUCE

2 tablespoons white sesame paste (tahini)

4 tablespoons castor sugar

4 teaspoons mirin

4 teaspoons soy sauce

4 tablespoons rice vinegar

ACCOMPANIMENTS

80g (2¾ oz) daikon, grated

4 chives, finely chopped

shichimi (Japanese seven-spice powder)

On a cold winter's day, a dish rich in protein, served steaming hot, brings a precious
feeling to the body and soul. Dishes are cooked for longer, sake is served hot, and even
fish have a higher fat content and a richer taste. In Japanese cuisine, there are several
styles of pot dishes, including sukiyaki, shabu-shabu and mizutaki. Sukiyaki is prepared
in a special iron pan at the table by cooking thinly sliced beef together with various
vegetables, beancurd and harusame (Japanese vermicelli). Shabu-shabu is prepared
in a special copper pan by cooking thinly sliced beef and various vegetables in boiling
water. It is served with a special white sesame sauce. Mizutaki literally means 'water-
simmered cooking'.

  Hot pot dishes are traditionally cooked at the table using a portable gas cooker or

hibachi. An earthenware claypot is used for this dish to keep it warm. There are various sizes of pots available, from small dishes for 1–2 people to large dishes for up to 8 people.

Reconstitute the dried shitake mushrooms by soaking them in some warm water for about 30 minutes or until the caps are soft. Cut and discard the stems and reserve the caps.

Bring a pot of water to the boil and add the harusame. Cook for 1 minute, then drain well and set aside.

To make the dipping sauce, whisk the sesame paste, sugar, mirin, soy sauce and rice vinegar in a bowl until well combined. Divide sauce among 4 bowls.

Arrange the momen-dofu, harusame, shitake mushrooms, takenoko, kombu, beef and shungiku in 4 small, heatproof ceramic pots. Pour the dashi into the 4 pots. Place each pot on a hibachi or portable stove, and bring to the boil.

Serve and eat over heat with dipping sauce and accompaniments on the side.

The
Japanese kitchen

Each Japanese kitchen has a different story and character, depending on the traditions that were handed down through the family that uses it, and the cooks who have used it.

Today, most Japanese kitchens do not differ greatly from the average western kitchen. Japanese kitchens usually contain some utensils, tableware and ingredients that would be familiar to many western cooks. However, many unique utensils and ingredients would also be found in addition to these, including the *sudare* (sushi mat), distinctive tableware, and unfamiliar ingredients, all of which are an important part of daily life in Japan.

Utensils

Houcho (Japanese Knives)

Knives are mainly divided into two types: double-edged (western-type) blades and single-edged (Japanese-type) blades (including Japanese Samurai swords). A Japanese knife has a single-edged blade with a very delicate tip, and gives a sharper result than a double-edged one. However, a Japanese knife needs more honing, as it loses its edge and gets rusty quite easily.

Professional Japanese chefs use a wide variety of knives. For cooking at home two or three types of Japanese knifes are sufficient. Pictured left (from left to right) are the *yanagiba-bocho* (sashimi slicing knife), the *usuba-bocho* (vegetable knife) and the *deba-bocho* (filleting knife).

Oroshigane (Grater)

A Japanese grater can be made of copper, plastic, aluminium, stainless steel or ceramic, and will have tiny dense edges on the surface. When using such a grater, especially when grating ginger and wasabi, move your hand in a circular motion.

Slicer or Mandolin

Mandolin slicers do the work more rapidly and accurately than knives. The mandolin has several blades, which are used for cutting julienne strips or slices of different sizes and thicknesses. Japanese cooks also use a spin slicer to reduce vegetables to hair-like shreds. When purchasing a slicer, choose one designed for safety.

Sudare or Makisu (Sushi Mat)

The *sudare* is a small mat made of narrow strips of bamboo, and it is vital for rolling sushi. Several sizes of *sudare* are available, from those that are wider than a whole *nori* sheet to small ones to those made of thicker bamboo strips that are used to shape rolled omelettes. After use, brush the mat thoroughly with a sponge and dry in bright sunlight. The larger mats are more versatile.

Saibashi (Long Chopsticks)

Saibashi are a pair of long chopsticks made of bamboo. Their length makes them ideal for use when deep-frying or for stirring hot dishes.

 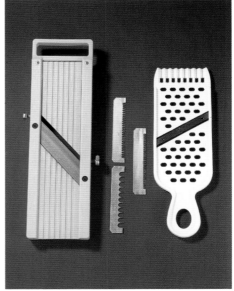

Rice Cooker

Rice used to be cooked in a heavy pot with a tight-fitting lid, but nowadays automatic electric or gas rice cookers are commonplace and do a wonderful job. Electric rice cookers with a keep-warm feature are also available.

Uroko-tori (Fish scaler)

The Japanese scaler (pictured left) has a thicker and rounder top than the western type, and is designed to cause less damage to the surface of the fish. To use the *uroko-tori*, draw it over the body of a fish, from tail to head, against the grain of the scales.

Hone-nuki (Tweezers)

Japanese tweezers have wide, flat tips designed to efficiently remove fish bones.

Suribachi and Surikogi (Mortar and Pestle)

An earthenware bowl with a wooden pestle that is used to pulverise ingredients such as sesame seeds. A feature of the Japanese grinding bowl is the inside surface, which has fine, sharp ridges to hold the seeds against the pestle. *Suribachi* are available in several sizes, but one about 20 cm (8 in) in diameter is sufficient for most grinding. A blender can also be used.

Hangiri (Sushi Bowl)

This wide, flat-bottomed wooden vessel is used for combining cooked rice with a vinegar mixture to make sushi rice. The wood absorbs excess moisture and the large surface area allows the rice to cool rapidly, which gives it a glossy sheen. A large wooden salad bowl can be substituted. To make enough rice to serve three or four people, a tub about 50 cm (20 in) in diameter is required. Before using, wipe the inside thoroughly with a cloth dipped in a mixture of vinegar and water to prevent the rice sticking to the inside.

Hibachi (Charcoal Burner)

In Japan, the hibachi was the main source of winter heating before gas and kerosene heaters came into general use. It was also the main device for cooking, especially for stewing. The hibachi can be made of wood, bronze, iron, brass, copper or porcelain. Recently, hibachi have assumed a more decorative role at the table. When purchasing, check that the hibachi you buy can be used as a practical utensil.

Katanuki (Vegetable Cutters)
Many varieties of vegetable cutters are available in Japan. Specialty kitchenware shops may also carry a range of cutters. If unavailable, use metal cookie cutters instead. Slice the vegetable thinly first. Place the slices on a wooden board (harder surfaces could damage the edge of the cutters), and push the cutter through to cut out a shape. The type of vegetables you can use depends on the size of the cutters.

Tableware

A distinguishing feature of Japanese cuisine is the beauty of the tableware itself. Japanese people love the warmth of wood, and cherish its pleasant feel against the skin and its comfortable weight in the hands. The hard, cold chill of metal is not congenial to the traditional Japanese way of eating with bowl in one hand and chopsticks in the other, even though metal bowls were introduced to Japan as early as the eighth century.

Increasing industrialisation in the Meiji and Tasiho periods (1867–1925) affected the manufacture of porcelain and glass, making mass-produced, cheap wares available to all. Traditional lacquerware, impossible to mass produce, was priced out of competition and slowly faded from the market. Nowadays, there is keen interest in traditional, quality Japanese kitchenware.

Bowls

Bowls are made of lacquer, urethane, ceramic, china, glass, wood or bamboo. They are used for soups, rice, dipping sauces, dishes or desserts.

Plates

Japanese plates are usually ceramic, china, lacquer, urethane or glass. They are designed for serving several dishes together.

Chopsticks and Chopstick Pillows

Japanese chopsticks (hashi) are made of many different materials and also come in a variety of sizes. The sizes may depend on the diner's age and gender, and on the formality of the occasion. There are some specialised chopsticks such as those with a 'stopper' to use when eating slippery food or with a device to allow for easier eating. Disposable chopsticks, usually made of wood or bamboo waste, are used at many restaurants. Chopstick pillows are small, attractive pieces of porcelain that diners use to rest their chopsticks on when they are not in use. Small pebbles or shells can also work well.

Teapots and Teacups

Teapots (kyūsa) for brewing tea come in a huge range of sizes, shapes and materials. Most teapots are ceramic or porcelain, though nowadays even glass and aluminium may be used. Many teapots are designed to retain tea leaves inside the teapot when the tea is being poured into cups. Japanese teacups (yunomi) do not have handles.

Groceries

Aonori (Green Seaweed Flakes)

Aonori is dried seaweed, flaked into small pieces. It is sold in packets or jars at Asian or Japanese food stores. It is sprinkled over food just before serving. Choose dark green flakes.

Japanese Azuki (Adzuki or Red Beans)

Several types of small red beans are used in Japanese desserts. They are also available in glaze form (*amanatto*) or in a paste. Japanese sweet cakes and confectionery mostly use a sweet azuki (red bean) paste as a filling. These cakes contain sweetness with less fat and protein than the many desserts throughout the western world, which rely on animal fats including butter and eggs.

Bainiku (Ume-boshi Purée)

Bainiku is a purée of *ume-boshi* (Japanese pickled plum). It is used as a topping and a dip, or in dressings. It is available from Japanese food shops in a bottle or a tube.

Domyoji-ko (Steamed and Roasted Sticky Rice)

Used in Japanese desserts, domyoji-ko is readily available at Japanese grocery shops.

Gari (Sliced Ginger in Vinegar)

A condiment served with sushi. To make gari, young ginger is peeled, sliced thinly, blanched and pickled in a sweet vinegar.

Goma (Sesame Seeds)

Nutty-flavoured, oil-rich little black or white seeds that are used roasted or unroasted in Japanese cooking. Seeds are sprinkled over the finished dish or ground into sauces and dressings. Ground sesame paste (*goma dare*) is available in tubes. Sesame salt (*goma shio*) is a mixture of well-ground sesame seeds and salt, used as a condiment.

Hoba (Ficus lyrata Leaf)

An inedible leaf, used dried to wrap beef or fish before cooking. The leaf imparts a strong aroma to meat when cooked on the hibachi (a small charcoal burner). Cut fresh leaves into approximately 15 cm x 30 cm (6 in x 12 in) pieces and dry in the shade. It is best to buy the whole plant from a nursery and cultivate the plant to harvest the leaves as you need them.

Kanpyo (Dried Gourd Shavings)

Kanpyo *is* made from the cream-coloured flesh of the white-flowered gourd (*yūgao*). The pith is shaved into very long, thin strips and dried. It is used as a filling in sushi rolls and also in soups, and as an edible tie or string for food. It is sold in packets in Japanese food shops.

Kanten (Agar-agar)

A gelatin-like substance that is used as a setting agent. It is made from several varieties of red seaweed and melts at a higher temperature than gelatin, and so is more useful in hot weather. Agar-agar is sold in strands or as a powder in Asian food shops.

Katakuriko (Potato Starch)

Katakuriko is a special potato starch. It is sold in packets in Japanese food shops and is used to thicken soups or sauces, and added to tempura flour to give a crispy result.

Katsuo-bushi (Dried Bonito Flakes)

The bonito is a member of the mackerel family. Dried bonito fillets are shaved into translucent flakes to be sprinkled on food just before serving. Along with kombu (kelp), katsuo-bushi is an indispensable ingredient in dashi, the basic Japanese soup stock. Dried bonito flakes are sold in packets in Asian and Japanese food shops.

Kombu (Dried Kelp)

Kombu (or *konbu*) is rich in glutamic acid, calcium, iodine and iron. It is one of the basic ingredients of Japanese stocks used in Japanese cooking. After wiping kombu with a wet cloth, add to boiling water to make a kombu stock. It can also be deep-fried. Kombu is sold in packets in Asian and Japanese food shops. Keep in an airtight container once the packet has been opened.

Kome (Japonica Short-grain Rice)

Japonica short-grain rice has a more rounded shape than long-grain rice varieties such as jasmine rice. When Japonica rice is cooked with water, it becomes slightly gluey in texture and the grains cling together. This is ideal for Japanese cuisine.

Komezu (Rice Vinegar)

Komezu is suitable for Japanese cuisine, especially for making sushi rice. It tastes a little like white vinegar, but it has a thicker consistency. White vinegar is a suitable substitute, but it is worth finding the real thing if possible.

Kuzu (Kuzu Starch)

A high-quality thickener made from the kuzu potato. It is similar to katakuriko, but once kuzu has melted and set, it keeps its shape, unlike katakuriko. It is used to thicken soups or stews, and in desserts or dumplings as a wrapper. It is available from Japanese grocery shops.

Midori (Japanese Liqueur)

A Japanese liqueur flavoured with honeydew melon. It has a distinctive intense emerald green colour. Midori is quite sweet, so it is good as an apéritif or a digestif.

Mirin (Sweet Cooking Rice Wine)

Mirin gives a glossy appearance and a slightly sweet taste to food. When grilling, brush mirin over an ingredient for a nice golden colour. When stewing, add a little mirin to enhance the taste.

Miso (Fermented Soybean Paste)

Miso is a very flavoursome ingredient. 'White' and 'red' varieties are available, but the colour may range from dark brown to creamy gold. (The colour depends on the length of fermentation.) The lighter varieties tend to be less salty and sweeter than the darker varieties. White miso is more popular for soups, sauces and seasoning.

Nori (Roasted Seaweed Sheet)

Nori is used to make sushi rolls. It is usually sold toasted or untoasted, in a cellophane or plastic bag. Once opened, store in an air-tight container or use straight away. If you purchase untoasted nori, lightly toast each sheet over an open flame before using.

Sake (Japanese Rice Wine)

Sake is made from fermented rice that is brewed and matured. It has a huge range of flavours and can be dry or sweet. Sake can be served either hot or cold, depending on the season and the style of sake. Naturally, cooking sake is cheaper than drinking sake, and the two are not really interchangeable, but if you have left-over sake, it can be used for cooking. When used in cooking, a small amount of sake enhances the flavour of other ingredients.

Sansho (Japanese Pepper Tree)

The leaves and berries of the sansho tree are used in Japanese cooking. Dried and finely ground sansho berries have a fragrant aroma and a sharp taste that is used in cooked dishes such as barbecued eel. The fresh leaves are used in clear Japanese soups and salads. Sansho pepper is sold in small bottles in Japanese food stores.

Shichimi (Japanese Seven-spice Powder)

A blend of seven spices or herbs including chilli, Japanese pepper, rapeseed, citrus zest and other ingredients that vary depending on the spice seller. It is served with sauces or noodles.

Shitake Mushrooms

These are available fresh or dried, but only extra-fresh shitake can be eaten raw. Dried ones need to be soaked and cooked in one of the Japanese stocks. Dried shitake contains more vitamins and aroma than the fresh. Leave them in strong sunlight for 30 minutes before soaking, as this will concentrate the flavour.

Shoyu (Japanese Soy Sauce)

Made from a fermented mixture of brine, wheat, malt and soybeans, Japanese soy sauce is slightly different from Chinese soy sauce. There are three types of soy sauce: koi-kuchi (dark soy), usu-kuchi (light soy), which is saltier, and others designed for particular dishes. For sashimi, use either koi-kuchi, tamari (thickened soy sauce) or sashimi-jyoyu (sashimi soy sauce).

Takuan (Pickled Daikon)

Pickled daikon comes in two colours, white or yellow, and can be sweet or salty. After drying the daikon under sunlight, it is pickled in salt and turmeric is added to colour it a bright yellow. The texture is crunchy and the taste is pungent. It is available in a plastic packets at Asian food shops.

Tofu (Beancurd)

Two main kinds of tofu are used: momen-dofu, which has a firm texture, and kinugoshi-dofu, which has a much finer and softer texture. Momen-dofu is good for cooking, as it won't fall apart easily. Kinugoshi-dofu is eaten raw in summer or as yudo-fu, which is tofu cooked in boiling water in a flat-bottomed pot and served with a dipping sauce. Check the date on the packet and choose the freshest one from the refrigerated section of your Asian supermarket.

Ugo (Seaweed)

An edible red or green thin seaweed, usually sold salted in a packet. Before using *ugo*, it should be rinsed under running water to remove excess salt, and squeezed dry. *Ugo* is served with sashimi or salad.

Ume-boshi with Shiso (Dried, Salted Pickled Japanese Plum with Shiso)

The Japanese plum *ume-boshi* can be large or small, hard or soft. It is usually pickled with salt and coloured red by being preserved in red *shiso* leaves in a dark place for almost a year. It tastes much too salty to eat a whole large one, but it is good when combined with other ingredients and is used in pastes, dressings and sauces. The paste of *ume-shiso* purée (*shiso-ume*) is available from Japanese food shops in tubes or bottles.

Wasabi (Japanese Horseradish)

Wasabi powder and paste are well known, because they are convenient and inexpensive. The recipes in this book use wasabi paste sold in tubes. Fresh wasabi may be available at specialist grocers. It has a great texture and aroma and an extremely hot taste.

Yukari (Salted Red Shiso)

The rough-grained, dried red leaves of *shiso* (prickly ash) can be preserved in salt, resulting in a salty, sour condiment. It is popular in Japanese cuisine, sprinkled on rice or salads. It is sold in packets or bottles at Asian grocery shops.

Yuzu (Japanese Citron)

Only the zest or juice of *yuzu* is used as a condiment. The fresh zest can be sliced or grated into soups, sauces or salads. It has a delicate citrus aroma in winter. The juice is more sour than sweet, and is ideal in dressings and in combination with other ingredients. If not available fresh, dried or frozen yuzu is available from Japanese grocery stores.

Yuzu Miso

A combination of miso and grated yuzu zest, *yuzu miso* is used to thicken sauces. It is available in packets from Japanese grocery stores.

Vegetables and fruits

Benishoga
Benishoga is young ginger that is salted and pickled in vinegar with red shiso or artificial colouring. It is sold sliced or shredded and is often used as a garnish. Benishoga is saltier than gari, the pickled pink ginger often served with sushi.

Daikon (Giant White Radish)
Daikon is used in stews, salads, as a condiment or pickle, and raw in sliced, grated or carved forms. Select daikon that has dense, tight flesh and no surface wrinkles (it has a milder flavour).

Enoki Mushrooms
These creamy-coloured mushrooms have long, thin stems and tiny caps (see photo 1). Wrapped in paper and refrigerated, they will keep well for a couple of days.

Hakusai (Chinese Cabbage)
One of the many varieties of Chinese cabbage, hakusai has a very high water content. It is often used in Japanese salads, pickles and stews.

Kaki (Persimmon)
There are two varieties of this autumn fruit. One type can be eaten raw, straight from the tree, and the other type needs to ripen after being harvested. The most readily available, orange-coloured persimmon can be eaten when the flesh is soft and the colour intensely orange.

Kaiware (Radish Sprouts)
The taste of kaiware is similar to mustard cress, but the sprouts are longer (about 15 cm/6 in). Choose sprouts with crispy stems. They are used in salads and as a garnish.

1   2

3   4

Kinome (Prickly Ash Leaves)

The young leaves of sansho (prickly ash tree) (see photo 2 on page 41), are used as a garnish. They can also be braised or made into a paste to impart a unique aromatic flavour.

Kuri (Chestnuts)

Chestnuts are in season in autumn, when they can be consumed raw. Frozen or bottled chestnuts can also be used, but dried chestnuts are not suitable for Japanese cooking.

Kyūri (Cucumber)

Japanese cucumbers are less watery than English cucumbers and measure about 20 cm (8 in) long. Lebanese cucumbers are similar to the Japanese variety and can be substituted.

Mitsuba (Trefoil)

With a taste somewhere between celery and parsley, mitsuba (see photo 3 on page 41) is used in soups, sushi, salads and for garnish. Choose small leaves with a softer texture.

Myoga (Myoga Ginger)

Myoga is in season from late spring to summer. Only buds and stems are eaten. Unlike the root, it is not hot. It is used in salads, sushi, soups, sashimi or as a garnish. (See photo 4 on page 41).

Nanohana (Canola or Rape)

The edible yellow flowers of nanohana are produced in spring and are a popular garnish. The stems, leaves and flowers are used in salads, tempura and pickles.

Nashi (Chinese Pear or Apple Pear)

Unlike regular pears, nashi are low in acid and aroma and are quite hard even when ripe. They are rounded like an apple, and much crunchier and juicier than regular pears.

Renkon (Lotus Root)

Renkon is a rhizome with a crisp texture. A decorative pattern is revealed when it is sliced (see photo 1 on page 42). Peel, slice and boil them in water with a few drops of vinegar to keep the white colour. Fresh renkon is preferable to the frozen, canned or dried varieties.

Satoimo (Taro)

Unlike the common potato, *satoimo* has a hairy brown skin and a slimy texture that remains after cooking. Small satoimo weighing less than 100g (3½ oz) each are best. They are used in stews or soups. They are sometimes labelled as a type of yam.

Shimeji Mushrooms

Shimeji mushrooms (see photo 2 on page 42), have a delightful taste but only a mild aroma. The fat caps and stems are used in soups, grills and tempura.

Shiso

Shiso (see photo 3 on page 42), is readily available in summer, in green and red varieties. Red shiso leaves are used mostly to give colour to pickles, especially ume-boshi (pickled plum). Green shiso is used as a garnish in salads, sashimi or sushi for its distinctive aroma.

Shungiku (Garland or Spring Chrysanthemum)

The leaves of shungiku have a strong aroma and a distinctive flavour, and are used as a vegetable in hotpots and tempura, and fresh or blanched in a salad.

Takenoko (Bamboo Shoots)

Takenoko are used in stews, tempura or soups and are available in spring. Remove the husks and cook until soft. (Soak large shoots in water overnight with a teaspoonful of baking soda first.) Pre-cooked bamboo shoots are also available in vacuum packs.

Wasabi (Japanese Horseradish)

Fresh *wasabi* (see photo 4 on page 44), has lovely texture and aroma, and an extremely hot taste. It is superior to the powders and pastes sold pre-made, but is not readily available outside Japan.

Basics

Basic recipes

Dashi (stock)

Dashi is Japan's fundamental stock and seasoning, much used in Japanese cooking as a base and for soup. When well made, dashi has a wonderful aroma and goes particularly well with Japanese clear soup (suimono). The dipping sauce for tempura is based on stock made with dashi.

Katsuo-bushi (dried bonito flakes), kombu (kelp) and shīˉtake mushrooms are used for dashi. Other ingredients, such as small dried prawns (shrimps), small fish (for example, dried anchovies) or fish or chicken bones are also sometimes used. The use of kombu dashi and shīˉtake dashi indicates ancient Buddhist influences, which preclude the use of animal parts in cooking.

Dashi is known to contain umami (deliciousness), a feature much prized in Japanese cooking. Umami is a Japanese word meaning 'savoury', 'deliciousness', 'rich' or 'the scale of deliciousness that measures the taste of glutamate'. Umami was identified in 1908 by Kikunae Ikeda as the fifth primary taste after sweetness, bitterness, saltiness and sourness. Mrs Ikeda discovered that the glutamic acid in kelp stock emphasised the deliciousness of other ingredients. In the west it is known as monosodium glutamate, which is used as a flavour enhancer in cooking.

To make dashi, dried bonito flakes, kelp or shîtake mushrooms are placed in boiling water and simmered very gently to extract the full true flavour of the base ingredient. The stock is then sieved, and used according to the recipe.

Katsuo (bonito) dashi

Freshly shaved dried bonito (katsuo-bushi) is used to make this standard stock for soups and sauces. The 'first' Katsuo Dashi has an incomparable aroma and is often used in clear soups and miso soups. The second dashi has a weaker flavour and is often used in stews, or combined with other stocks. The dipping sauce for tempura also uses Katsuo Dashi.

makes 4 cups (1 litre/2 pints)

8 cups (2 litres/4 pints) water
50g (1¾ oz) katsuo-bushi (dried bonito) shavings

To make the first Katsuo Dashi, bring 4 cups (1 litre/2 pints) of water to the boil and add the katsuo-bushi shavings. When the katsuo-bushi shavings float to the surface, remove from heat.

Drain the Katsuo Dashi into a pot. Set aside. Keep the katsuo-bushi shavings for the second stock. To make the second Katsuo Dashi, use the leftover shavings from the first dashi and repeat with another 4 cups (1 litre/2 pints) of water. Keep the stocks separate. Depending on the dish you intend to make, use one stock and keep the other refrigerated in a ceramic or glass bottle (it will only keep for a couple of days).
Kombu (Kelp) Dashi

.

Kombu (kelp) dashi

Though less fragrant than Katsuo Dashi, Kombu Dashi contributes greatly as a flavour enhancer because of the very high amount of natural monosodium glutamate it contains. It is used in almost all Japanese food, often in combination with bonito stock

makes 4 cups (1 litre/2 pints)

50 g (1¾ oz) kombu (kelp)
4 cups (1 litre/2 pints) water

Wipe the kombu lightly with a dry kitchen towel. Combine the kombu and water and bring to boil. When the water boils, remove the pan from the heat, and remove the kombu from the stock.

Shitake mushroom dashi

This flavoursome stock is used in stews or soups and is particularly useful for cooking vegetarian dishes.

makes 4 cups (1 litre/2 pints)

12 dried shitake mushrooms
4 cups (1 litre/2 pints) cold water

Place shitake mushrooms and cold water in a saucepan. Soak for 30 minutes, then bring to the boil. When the water boils, remove the pan from the heat and strain. Use the liquid as stock and retain the mushrooms for use in another dish.

SEASONED DASHI

You can combine one type of dashi with another and add seasonings to impart extra flavour to stews and other dishes. Seasoned/mixed dashi can be made ahead of time and stored in the refrigerator for up to 2 days.

makes 2 cups (500 ml/ 16 fl oz)

1 cup (250 ml/8 fl oz) Katsuo Dashi (see page 50)
1 cup (250 ml/8 fl oz) Kombu Dashi (See page 51)
1 tablespoon soy sauce
1 tablespoon mirin

Combine Katsuo Dashi and Kombu Dashi in a saucepan and simmer gently until warm. Do not boil. Add the soy sauce and mirin, mix well and remove the pan from the heat.

Other basic recipes

Japanese-style omelette

Serves 2

4 eggs
2 tablespoons super dashi
1 tablespoon caster sugar
1 tablespoon mirin
1 teaspoon light colour soy sauce
1 tablespoon vegetable oil
1 tablespoon grated daikon
radish or red radish
soy sauce

Crack eggs into a bowl and add super dashi, caster sugar, mirin and soy sauce then whisk. Strain into another bowl.

Place a non-stick frying pan over a medium heat for 1 minute. Pour in a little oil and swirl evenly over the pan.

Pour in one third of the egg mixture and cook until set around the edges.

With a spatula fold one third towards the front of the pan, then fold over again in the same direction onto the remaining portion.

Add a little more oil to the pan and pour half of the remaining egg mixture onto the empty area of the pan and cook until the edge sets.

Again fold one third towards the folded egg, then fold this over on top of previous roll, making a flat roll on one side of the pan.

Add more oil and pour in the remaining egg mixture, and repeat the folding process. With the spatula, give a little push to mould the shape.

When cooked, remove from the heat, and place on a bamboo mat on a dry surface. Wrap the omelette with the bamboo mat and shape. By pressing with your fingers on one side only along the length of the roll, you can make a wedge shape which produces attractive 'petals' when cut across the roll. It can also be left as a cylinder or squared off.

Cut into pieces. Serve with grated daikon and soy sauce.

SWEET RED BEANS

Red beans are an important ingredient in Japanese desserts, where they are often made into a paste or served whole. Red beans are high in protein and low in fat.

makes 1 quantity of cooked sweet red beans

1 cup (220 g/7 oz) raw red beans, rinsed and soaked in water for 4–5 hours (optional)
2 tablespoons castor sugar
a pinch of salt

Place the beans in a pan, add water to cover the beans 3 cm (1¼ in) above. Bring to the boil rapidly, over a high heat, with the lid on. Add 1 cup of cold water and bring it back to the boil. This is a traditional step believed to soften the skin of the bean. Remove from heat and drain.

Return the beans to the pan again and add water to cover the beans with 3 cm (1¼ in) of water above. Bring rapidly to the boil with the lid on, then simmer for a couple of

minutes. As before, add 1 cup of cold water, bring back to the boil, then remove from heat and drain.

For the third time, return the beans to the pan and add enough water to cover the beans to 3 cm (1¼ in) above. Bring to the boil over high heat, then lower heat and simmer for 50–60 minutes, until the beans become soft. If necessary, top up water to keep the beans covered.

Place a cotton cloth in a bowl, and tip in the red beans. Gently squeeze to extract excess water, taking care not to crush the beans. Transfer the beans to a pan and add the sugar and salt, stirring gently over a low heat until the sugar dissolves. Set aside to cool, then store chilled in the refrigerator until required.

EGG MIMOSA

Egg Mimosa is widely used in modern Japanese cooking. It is useful for adding texture to a dish and binding ingredients together.

makes 1 quantity (about 3 tablespoons)

1 hard-boiled egg

Shell the egg, remove the yolk and discard the white. Using a wooden spoon, gently push the yolk through a sieve into a bowl, to make a light, moist powder. During this process, the mass of the ingredient increases greatly.

Preparation techniques for fish and seafood

Three-piece Filleting Technique

1 whole salmon, 1.5–3 kg (3–6 lb)

Most salmon is sold cleaned. But if the fish still has its guts, make a slit from the tail to the head along the belly with a sharp knife and open. Pull out and discard the insides and rinse the cavity under running water. Scale the fish using a uroko-tori (Japanese fish scaler) if possible, as it causes less damage to the fish.

Wipe the fish dry so that it is easier to work with. Position the fish flat on a board with the tail on the right hand side If you are right-handed, and hold the fish with your left hand. Reverse if you are left-handed. Insert the knife at the top of the fish head, just behind the head bone, with the blade angled slightly toward the fish head. Following the natural curve of the cheek, continue slicing in one smooth stroke behind the gills to the depth of the backbone, until you reach the underside of the fish. Holding the knife flat and the blade facing away from the fish head, insert the knife into the very top ridge of the of the fish head just behind the head bone (as pictured below left). In

one swift movement, slice the knife diagonally through the fish with the knife kept flat along the back bone, allowing the knife to cut though the flesh of the belly edge too. Continue in a drawing motion until you reach the tail and the fillet is free. Set the fillet aside and turn the fish over, again placing the tail on the right hand side of the board. Repeat all steps as above, but when making the second cut (along the backbone), insert the knife point sideways at the underside edge rather than the top of the fish.

Place the fillets cut side up on the board. Holding the knife on a fairly flat angle, cut from the centre of the fillet to belly edge, removing lower belly parts (as pictured opposite, centre).

Place the fillet on the board, skin side down. Run your finger along the fillet to check for bones. Remove any bones with a pair of tweezers (as pictured opposite, right).

Wipe the knife clean. Hold onto the tail end of a fillet with one hand (your left if you are right-handed), skin side down. Insert the knife at a slight angle just above the skin at the tail end, and move the knife along the skin about 5 cm (2 in) into the fillet. Holding the fish firmly, remove the knife. Gently pull the free flesh back just enough to hold the knife vertically above the skin you've just cut free from the fish. Make a 2 cm (¾ in) incision into the skin, cutting lengthwise about 2 cm (½ in) from the tail edge. This will create a 'buttonhole' that runs parallel to the length of the fish. Insert your left thumb into the 'buttonhole' in order to prevent the slippery skin from moving. Hold the knife flat side facing up, and begin cutting from the tail end near the buttonhole, just above the skin. Keeping the knife held flat just above the skin, carefully slice towards the head end in one continuous movement to free the flesh from the skin. Repeat with the other fillet.

Sashimi Slicing Techniques

Sashimi slicing techniques vary according to the type of fish. Here are the two main techniques: hiki-zukuri and sogi-zukuri. For both, you will need a long fillet of fish that is 6 cm (2½ in) wide and a clean, wet cloth. Filleting techniques are presented on the opposite page.

HIKI-ZUKURI

This is a basic sashimi technique to slice fish into pieces 2.5 cm (1 in) thick.

Place the fillet on a chopping board and hold onto the fillet with your left hand (reverse if you are left-handed). With a sashimi (filleting) knife slice the fish into pieces 2.5 cm (1 in) wide. After each cut, slide the piece along the cutting board about 10 cm (4 in) away from the fillet. Arrange the pieces neatly in a layered row. Balance the layered pieces on the flat side of the knife and transfer to serving dishes.

Wipe the knife clean with the cloth.

SOGI-ZUKURI

Sogi-zukuri is a technique for sashimi and sushi tops. This slice is thinner than hikizukuri sashimi, so it creates a different sensation in the mouth.

Hold onto the thicker end of the fillet with your left hand (reverse if you are left-handed). Insert the sashimi knife at a 45-degree angle into the fish and slide the knife towards the left to make a thin slice about 1cm (½ in) wide. Slice the remaining fillet into 1cm (½ in) wide pieces.

Cleaning of Calamari, Squid and Cuttlefish

Hold the calamari or squid tube in one hand and with the other hand pull out the tentacles. The insides should come away with the tentacles. Cut off and discard the guts and ink sac. Pull out the hard 'bone' inside the body and discard. Reserve the tentacles—they are edible.

Dry the calamari or squid with a cloth or paper towel. Holding the body with one hand, grasp one flap and pull it away from the other. Remove the skin by carefully rubbing it away with a cloth. Rinse and wipe dry.

Place the calamari or squid on the board, and cut lengthwise through the tube to open it. Remove any dark parts inside. Turn over so that inside of the flesh is face down on the board.

Slice into thin julienne with a filleting knife or prepare for nigiri-zushi or cooking by making shallow diagonal cuts at 1cm (½ in) intervals along the surface. (Do not cut through.) Repeat with the opposite diagonal to create a crosshatch pattern.

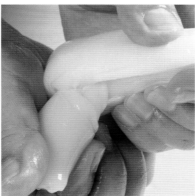

Preparation techniques for vegetables

Preparation of Vegetables for Stew

Pumpkins, turnips and carrots are fine examples of the kinds of vegetables that are suitable for Japanese stews. These vegetables hold their shape and texture throughout the cooking process, and look pleasing to the eye when served. Vegetables that flake after cooking, such as potatoes, are, therefore, not suitable.

SMALL VEGETABLES

This method works well for small vegetables that are best served whole, such as baby turnips, or very small satoimo.

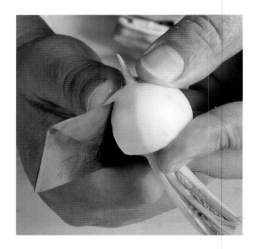

Hold the vegetable in one hand. Using a small knife, peel by making one cut from the stem to the bottom. Continue working around the vegetable working from top to bottom, keeping the width of the cuts as uniform as possible, and aiming to have all cuts meeting neatly at the bottom, in imitation of the vegetable's natural, round shape.

LARGE VEGETABLES WITH PEEL

This method is useful for large, thick-skinned vegetables that need to be cut into small pieces before they can be served, such as pumpkin. Many varieties of pumpkin have distinctly different coloured skin and flesh. With a little work you can accentuate this contrast and make a great visual addition to your dishes.

Begin with an unpeeled piece of pumpkin measuring 5 cm x 6 cm (2 in x 2½ in) across the surface of the skin. Neatly make a cut 1cm (½ in) away from the skin and slice off the flesh, leaving a piece of pumpkin 1cm (½in) thick with the skin still on. Place on a board with the skin facing up. With a small knife, trim the piece into a leaf shape as shown in the photo. Using the tip of the knife, draw a simple design on the surface of the skin, pressing hard enough to cut through the skin, but not into the flesh. Insert the knife below the skin and remove skin from within each shape outlined, leaving flesh showing through from beneath.

SHAPING WITH CUTTERS

This is the easiest way to create interesting shapes with vegetables. All you need are metal vegetable cutters; if they are unavailable, small cookie cutters can be substituted. Vegetables need to be chosen according to the size of the cutters.

Slice, but do not peel the vegetable. (The skin is cut off when you stamp out the shape with the cutter.) The thickness of the slices will depend on the type of vegetable you are cutting, but generally, between 3 mm–5 mm (⅛ in–⅛ in) is ideal. Place the slices on a wooden board (to avoid damaging cutters on a hard surface) and push the cutter through each slice.

Garnishes

Japanese cooking uses many garnish ideas to enhance the beauty of the cooked dish. Many of these ideas come from nature, and may vary according to the season. Popular motifs include flowers, leaves, birds or insects.

Once a vegetable is sliced, the moisture content evaporates quite quickly, leaving the vegetable dry and the juice weak. Keep the sliced vegetables in cold water until ready to use to avoid loss of flavour and moisture.

Shredded daikon

makes 1 quantity (about 60 g/2 oz)

1 daikon
iced water

Peel the daikon and cut out a 10 cm (4 in) cylinder. Holding the daikon in one hand, place the edge of the knife vertically on the daikon and move the knife in a sawing motion to 'peel' a continuous sheet of daikon of uniform thickness. Make a sheet of up to 10 cm (4 in) long.

Roll up the daikon gently without breaking, and cut into thin julienne. Soak in iced water until ready to use.

Harangiri

Harangiri is an inedible leaf carved with a small knife. It is a popular garnish in traditional Japanese cooking. Inexperienced cooks who are less skillful at carving and 'turning' with a knife, could use small cutter shapes instead. Bamboo, camellia and aspidistra leaves are all suitable for harangiri.

Using the tip of a small knife, on each leaf lightly draw the outline of a smaller leaf inside. Cut through the leaf along this outline, being careful to leave the outside edge intact.

CUCUMBER FAN

The cucumber fan epitomises the classic simplicity of Japanese shapes. It is found in most stylish and traditional Japanese restaurants. Unlike harangiri, this is an edible garnish.

makes 4 fans

1 large cucumber or 1 small winter melon

Using a small knife, cut the cucumber in half lengthways. Place the halved cucumber cut side down, leaving the skin intact. Cut both halves widthways into four 5 cm x 7 cm (2 in x 2¾ in) pieces. Remove the seeds in one neat cut, leaving 1 cm (½ in) flesh attached to the skin.

Using the tip of the knife, draw a fan shape over each skin. Trim, cutting cleanly to this outline. Using the knife tip, draw a design inside the fan, as shown in the

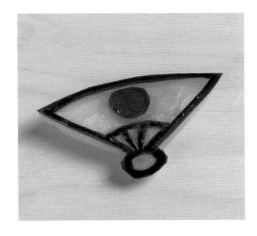

photo, pressing lightly to cut through the surface of the skin but not into the flesh, leaving a border about 2 mm wide around the edges. Insert the knife under each shape of the internal design and remove the skin in these areas to leave the white flesh showing from beneath, to form a pattern on the fan. Soak in water until ready for use.

CRANE

Like the cucumber fan, the crane is a beautiful, traditional and edible Japanese garnish.

makes 4 cranes

1 large cucumber or 1 small winter melon

As for the cucumber fan above, use a small knife and cut the cucumber in half lengthways. Place the halved cucumber cut side down, leaving the skin intact. Cut both halves widthways into four 5cm x 7cm (2 in x 2¾ in) pieces. Remove the seeds in one neat cut, leaving 1cm (½in) flesh attached to the skin.

Using the tip of a knife, draw a crane outline on the skin, as shown in the picture. Trim carefully to this shape, leaving the silhouette of the crane. Using the knife tip, draw a design on the 'body' as shown in the picture, pressing lightly to cut through the surface of the skin, but not into the flesh. Leave a border of skin approximately 2 mm wide around the edges. Insert the knife under each internal outline and carefully remove the skin from these areas, leaving the white flesh showing beneath, creating a pattern on the body. Soak in water until ready to use.

Sushi

Sushi

Suggested ingredients

For fillings try extra fresh fish such as salmon or tuna; smoked salmon; canned tuna mixed with mayonnaise; tempura; vegetables such as steamed asparagus or wilted English spinach; carrot sticks (or julienne of carrot) blanched in some boiling water to which a little sugar has been added; fresh salad leaves; avocado; fresh tomato; cheese or ham.

Suggestions for sauce

Soy sauce and wasabi are a basic combination. However, tamari (soy sauce without wheat) goes well with sashimi. If you like to have less salt on your food, choose salt-reduced soy sauce, or combine with super dashi to reduce saltiness. Or be innovative with sweet chilli sauce or a mixture of olive oil and soy sauce mixture.

Presentation

Depending on the occasion, sushi can be served in many different ways. It makes a perfect first course for Western-style dining, when it can be served on individual plates. For a large gathering it can be attractively displayed on large platters. Be imaginative with your decorations and garnishes.

Preparing sushi rice

4 cups rice, cooked

SUSHI VINEGAR MIXTURE
1 cup rice vinegar
3½ tablespoons caster sugar
a pinch salt

Equipment you will need:
- a wooden sushi bowl (or wooden salad bowl)
- a rice paddle (or a wooden spatula)
- hand fan or electric fan (or a piece of cardboard)
- muslin cloth or kitchen towel

Wipe the inside of the wooden bowl with a damp cloth to moisten. Transfer cooked rice from rice cooker into the centre of the sushi bowl.

Prepare the sushi vinegar mixture by combining all ingredients in a bowl.

Gradually pour sushi vinegar over slicing paddle across the bowl to break up lumps. Mix rice evenly around the bowl with a slicing action. While mixing, cool the rice with a hand fan. This helps rice absorb vinegar mixture and creates a glossy surface on rice.

When rice becomes lukewarm, cover with a damp muslin cloth.

Keep rice at room temperature. Do not refrigerate, as this dries out the sushi rice and causes the starch to break down.

To colour sushi rice, use beetroot juice or black (coloured) rice for natural colour.

SLENDER ROLL (HOSO-MAKI)

Makes 6 pieces.

This is the basic method for rolling up sushi. Once you master this, try large rolls and inside-out rolls.

1 nori sheet, halved crossways
1 cup sushi rice (page 70)
wasabi paste
¼ Lebanese cucumber, cut lengthwise, seeded and cut into long thin sticks
salt-reduced soy sauce
pickled ginger, optional
Use Te-zu (vinegar water) for handling rice, made by combining 1 cup of water with 1
    teaspoon rice vinegar.

ROLLING METHOD [right-handed]

Place bamboo mat on a board or other dry flat surface.
    Place half a sheet of nori on the mat, rough side up, one edge of the nori lining up with the front edge of the mat.
    Dip your right fingers into the vinegar water. With damp fingers, take sushi rice and spread evenly over ⅔ of the nori, leaving a space at the back edge. With your right index finger, draw a line of wasabi along the rice (photo 1).
    Place strips of cucumber side by side along the wasabi line (photo 2).
    Using both hands, lift the front edge of the mat and roll up to the end of the rice. While still wrapped, gently shape the roll, pushing rice in at both ends with fingertips (photo 3).
    Keep lifting up front edge of the bamboo mat as you roll the sushi on to the remaining uncovered portion of nori, giving a final light press on the edge before removing the mat completely (photo 4).

With a wet knife, slice the roll in half, then into thirds.
Serve with pickled ginger garnish and a dipping dish of soy sauce.

Spread rice with wet fingers, but do not splash nori.
For your first attempts at making sushi, keep fillings to a minimum for ease of rolling.
For more variety, you can make more sushi using other suitable fillings such as cooked
carrot sticks and asparagus.

INSIDE-OUT ROLL (HODAKA-MAKI)

Makes 8 pieces

1 sheet nori
1½ cups sushi rice (page 32)
wasabi paste
1 tablespoon Japanese mayonnaise
2 green salad leaves such as baby cos lettuce
2 large king prawns, cooked, peeled and deveined
2 stems of asparagus, cooked, lower portion removed
roasted white sesame seeds for decoration
Te-zu (vinegar water) for handling rice (see page 72)
a sheet of plastic wrap

Place nori on the bamboo mat. With wet fingers spread rice all over the nori (Page 76, photo 1).

Spread a piece of plastic wrap over the rice.

Place one hand on top of the plastic wrap, one hand underneath the mat and gently turn up side down. Remove the mat and place it underneath. The resulting arrangement is now the bamboo mat on the bottom, then the plastic wrap, rice and nori on top. With your finger, draw a thin line of wasabi and mayonnaise along the nori. Place salad leaves along the centre of the nori. Place the prawns and asparagus along the central area of the salad leaves (page 76, photo 2).

Using both hands (dry), roll up about two thirds of the way (page 76, photo 3).

Lift the mat and pull free the edge of the plastic wrap so it doesn't get caught in the roll. Roll the last bit, and remove the mat but not the plastic (page 76, photo 4).

With a sharp wet knife, cut in half and then quarters, making 8 pieces. Remove the plastic wrap. Decorate with roasted sesame seeds.

Other ingredients suitable for topping are roasted black sesame seeds, tobikko (flying fish roe) and egg mimosa (made by passing the yolk of a hardboiled egg through a sieve).

Large roll (futo-maki)

Makes 8 pieces

Futo-maki (literally 'fat roll') is a larger roll made using a whole nori sheet, a larger amount of rice and 3 to 6 fillings.

1 sheet nori
1½ cups sushi rice (see page 70)
wasabi paste
¼ Lebanese cucumber, cut lengthwise, seeded and cut into long thin sticks
¼ carrot, cut into lengthwise strips and cooked with a small amount of sugar for 5 minutes
1 Japanese omelette (see page 53), cut into strips
¼ grilled eel (Available in a vacuum-sealed packets from Japanese grocery shops. Cut off one strip about 1 cm wide along the length of the eel.)
soy sauce or salt-reduced soy sauce
pickled ginger, optional
Te-zu (vinegar water) for handling rice (see page 72)

Place the nori on the bamboo mat, and proceed as for the method for the slender roll (page 72).

A great variety of fillings can be used for these rolls, enabling you to vary the colours and textures. However, avoid fillings which are juicy, such as unseeded tomato. Suggested fillings are avocado, asparagus, green salad leaves and cooked poultry, beef or pork.

Hand-wrapped sushi roll

Serves 4

This is a great dish for informal occasions or summer Sunday lunches. Everyone can sit around the table and make their own sushi from a platter of pre-prepared ingredients.

4 cups sushi rice (page 70)
4 sheets of nori, cut into quarters
wasabi paste
Japanese mayonnaise

ANY SELECTION OF THE FOLLOWING FILLINGS:
4 fresh salmon slices, sushi-sliced
½ Lebanese cucumber, sliced in quarters, seeded and cut lengthwise into thin sticks
4 small green salad leaves
½ avocado, peeled and sliced
100g (4 oz) can of tuna, mixed with 1 tablespoon Japanese mayonnaise
¼ carrot, peeled and cut into thin strips
4 asparagus, cooked, lower section cut off
2 shiso leaves
processed cheese, cut into thin sticks
100g (4oz) grilled eel, sliced
salmon caviar, optional
reduced-salt soy sauce

Prepare all the ingredients on a plate and put rice in a bowl.

In your left hand hold a sheet of nori and with a wet spoon put sushi rice in the centre.

Add a little wasabi and mayonnaise to taste. Place on top any combination of the fillings.

With your right hand wrap up the nori, making a cone shape.

Spoon caviar on top.

Serve with soy sauce.

Many other ingredients can be included on the platter such as ham strips, tempura, grilled chicken or beef strips, prawns or smoked salmon.

Hand-ball sushi

Kids love this bite-sized sushi. It is a good choice for an o-bento lunch box.

1 egg, beaten with 1 teaspoon mirin and
a pinch salt
vegetable oil
1 cuttlefish
1 king prawn, cooked, peeled,
deveined and butterflied

1 slice smoked salmon
1 small slice proscuitto
2 cups sushi rice (page 70)
wasabi paste
soy sauce
5 sheets of plastic wrap, about 10 cm

To make thin egg omelette, heat a non-stick frying pan over moderate heat. Pour in
a little vegetable oil. Lower heat, pour egg mixture into pan and tilt quickly to spread
evenly over the bottom. When the surface of the egg is almost dry, use a spatula to
loosen edges and then insert spatula under and carefully flip the omelette. Cook for 10
seconds more and remove from pan onto a dry board. Cut into 2 cm-wide ribbons.

To prepare cuttlefish, discard bone, peel the skin off with fingers, and rinse. Blanch in
boiling water. With a knife, open and slice as for sushi topping (see page 52).

Lay a sheet of plastic wrap on a board and place an ingredient, such as king prawn,
cut side up on the centre.

Top with an amount of rice about the size of a golf ball. Draw edges of plastic wrap
over rice and prawn, while twisting together and shape into a ball.

Repeat with other ingredients.

Just before serving, remove plastic wrap and decorate with a small amount of wasabi
and nori threads.

Serve with soy sauce.

Hand-moulded sushi (nigiri-zushi)

Makes 22 pieces, sufficient for 2 main meal servings

2 cups sushi rice (including rice in cucumber roll) (page 72)

2 green king prawns

2 slices salmon sushi

2 slices tuna sushi

2 slices cuttlefish

2 slices king fish sushi

1 stuffed green olive, cut in half

2 stems of snow pea sprout

2 snow peas, blanched

wasabi paste

4 pieces cucumber sushi roll (page 72)

2 slices of egg omelette (page 82),

pickled ginger for garnish

soy sauce

Te-zu (vinegar water) for handling rice (see page 72)

TO PREPARE GREEN KING PRAWNS

green king prawns

bamboo skewers

1 cup rice vinegar

½ cup water

2 tablespoons caster sugar

Rinse prawns. To keep prawns from curling during parboiling, pierce with skewers along the belly side from head to tail.

Bring water to boil in a saucepan and add a pinch of salt. Simmer prawns for 3 minutes over moderate heat, then plunge into cold water.

Remove skewers. Remove shells from prawns, but leave tails intact. De-vein.

Make a slit on the belly side to open up like a butterfly. Then gently flatten out.

Combine vinegar, water, sugar and place prawns in this mixture until ready to use.

NIGIRI TECHNIQUE METHOD

Have the sliced and other ingredients ready. Place a dry board on the kitchen bench.

Moisten hand with the vinegar water and pick up about 1 tablespoonful rice. Form into a ball, pressing gently with the hand but do not squash. Pick up a sushi slice with your other hand and spread on a dab of wasabi with one finger of the hand holding the rice (photo 1, opposite).

Place rice on the sushi slice and with index and middle fingers press firmly to form a mounded shape (photo 2).

Roll sushi over and press again with two fingers against the fish (photo 3).

Rotate sushi 180° and press again with two fingers against the fish (photo 4).

Arrange on a platter with sushi rolls and slices of omelette. Garnish with pickled ginger; serve with soy sauce.

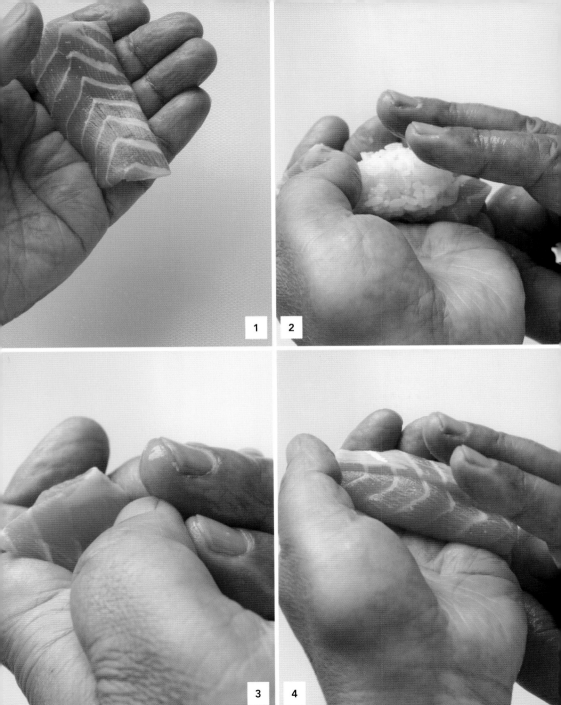

TOFU-POUCH SUSHI (INARI-ZUSHI)

Makes 6 pieces

This is popular for picnic lunches, particularly served in combination with other sushi such as cucumber rolls.

tofu (bean curd) pouches (abura-gea), available from Asian grocery stores
2 dried shiitake mushrooms, soaked in water for at least 15 minutes and chopped finely
¼ small carrot, peeled and chopped finely
1 cup super dashi (page 66)
½ cup soy sauce
2 tablespoons mirin
1 tablespoon caster sugar
3 cups sushi rice (page 18)
cucumber roll to accompany (page 72)
soy sauce
saucepan lid or saucer or sheet of foil smaller than size of saucepan to be used

PREPARATION OF BEAN CURD POUCHES

To remove the excess oil from the bean pouches, place the pouches in boiling water and leave for a minute, then drain and squeeze out the water and unwanted oil.

Place bean curd pouches, shiitake mushrooms and carrot in a saucepan. Add dashi, soy sauce, mirin and caster sugar. To keep bean curd submerged while cooking, place a smaller lid or saucer on top. Bring the mixture to the boil and simmer over low heat for about 10 minutes. Remove from heat and allow to stand until liquid is cool.

Remove bean curds and squeeze to remove excess water. Transfer to cutting board and cut each in half to make two pouches. Set aside.

Mix the shiitake and carrots into sushi rice with a rice paddle.

Carefully open the bean curd pouch. With wet fingers, make a small ball of rice and place it into the pouch. Press sides with fingers to make a pillow shape. Tuck ends of pouch inside. Repeat with the other pouches.

Arrange on a platter with cucumber roll. Serve with soy sauce.

Present these sushi in an o-bento box with cucumber rolls and a small container of soy sauce.

Roasted black sesame seeds can be sprinkled over the rice before tucking in the flap of the tofu pouch.

Seasoned, pre-cooked bean curd pouches are available from Japanese or Asian grocery shops.

Leave some pouches open to vary presentation.

Scattered sushi (chirashi-zushi)

This is a dish for celebrating the change of season, and for happy occasions. Typically sushi rice is mixed with various ingredients, then topped with seasonal vegetables, fish or egg. Other traditional ingredients are seasoned kampyo strips, shredded thin omelette, snow peas and grilled eel. More recently, corn, blueberries, or even tempura may be added for extra colour. It may be served in a large bowl, individual bowls or even a box.

¼ daikon radish, sliced
½ cup rice vinegar
¼ cup water
1 teaspoon caster sugar
2 dried shiitake, soaked in water at least
  15 minutes
1 cup super dashi
1 tablespoon caster sugar
1 tablespoon soy sauce
1 tablespoon mirin

2 stems Chinese broccoli
4 green king prawns, heads removed,
  deveined and rinsed
2 cups cooked sushi rice (page 72)
2 hard-boiled egg yolks, sieved
  (egg mimosa)
½ cup fresh or frozen green peas, cooked
4 tablespoons salmon caviar
wasabi paste
soy sauce

To make pickled daikon flowers, cut daikon slices with a flowershaped cutter. Soak slices in a mixture of ¼ cup rice vinegar, ¼ cup water and 1 teaspoon caster sugar mixture for 30 minutes.

To prepare shiitake, discard the stems and slice. Put dashi-stock, caster sugar, soy sauce and mirin in a saucepan; add shiitake slices. Simmer for 10 to 15 minutes over low heat.

Blanch Chinese broccoli for 1 minute and drain. Cook king prawns in salted water for 2 minutes, then drain.

Squeeze shiitake mushrooms to remove excess liquid and mix with sushi rice. Place

sushi rice into individual bowls or one large bowl.

Sprinkle egg mimosa and green peas over the top. Decorate with broccoli, king prawn and salmon caviar set on pickled daikon flower.

Serve with wasabi and soy sauce.

DIPPING SAUCES

Dipping sauces are available at Asian groceries, but they are easy to make if you wish to make your own

They can be made well ahead and stored in airtight containersin the refrigerator for a couple of days.

Sashimi

Sashimi

Sashimi means 'sliced raw fish'. Although this is a simple dish to prepare since it needs no cooking, great care needs to be taken about the selection of fresh fish. Since the freshness of the fish is paramount, it may be worthwhile enlisting the services of a reliable fishmonger to make your selection. These days fishmongers are well aware of the special requirements of sashimi. White-fleshed fish are more favoured as a summer dish, while red-fleshed fish seems to be preferred in the colder seasons.

It is a good idea to take a portable ice-box with you when purchasing fish for sashimi. Store the fish in the refrigerator, covered with cling film. It is best eaten the same day as purchased.

When slicing, use a chopping board that has been washed properly and disinfected by sunlight. A sharp knife is necessary for slicing, to prevent breaking the texture of the flesh.

Soy sauce with wasabi is the standard dipping sauce, and grated daikon or ginger are good additional condiments. Vinegar with soy sauce and hot mustard can also be used.

Basic sashimi

serves 2

This simple dish of tuna sashimi is served on a bed of fine daikon strips which can be dipped in soy and eaten along with the tuna.

a block of tuna fillet, approx. 300 g (11 oz)
¼ daikon radish, peeled
wasabi paste
tamari or salt-reduced soy sauce

Slice tuna fillet into sashimi.

Preparation of daikon

Traditionally the daikon garnish is prepared by peeling it off in a continuous sheet.

Start by peeling and cutting out a 10cm cylinder of fresh daikon. Holding the daikon in one hand, place the edge of the knife vertically on the daikon and cut in a sawing motion to peel a continuous sheet.

Carefully roll up the sheet, and cut into thin julienne. Soak in iced water until ready to use.

This may be rather difficult for novices. Try using a vegetable peeler or Japanese-style slicer (available from Japanese, Chinese or Korean shops) or a mandolin to slice off thin daikon strips. Then roll up and cut into thin julienne as before.

Place sliced tuna on top of the prepared daikon and serve with wasabi paste and tamari or salt-reduced soy sauce.

JAPANESE-STYLE BEEF CARPACCIO

Serves 4

RICE VINEGAR MIXTURE
½ cup rice vinegar
1 tablespoon caster sugar
a pinch of salt

¼ brown onion, thinly sliced and soaked
in water
400 g (14 oz) beef sirloin or rump steak (in
one piece)

DRESSING
1 tablespoon light colour soy sauce

1 teaspoon grape seed oil or extra virgin
olive oil
1 tablespoon rice vinegar
1 clove garlic, grated (or chopped
fresh chilli if you prefer)
1 very small knob fresh ginger, grated
1 teaspoon sake
1 teaspoon caster sugar

shiso leaves or any green salad leaves
1 lime, thinly sliced

Combine all the ingredients for rice vinegar mixture in a bowl.

Drain onion and place in the mixture.

Heat up a frying pan over a high heat. Cook the beef until all surfaces turn light
brown. Transfer into iced water for 3 seconds. Drain and pat dry with kitchen paper.

Place beef in the vinegar mixture and refrigerate for 20–30 minutes.

Meanwhile, mix all dressing ingredients in a bowl and set aside.

Remove the beef from the vinegar mixture and transfer to a chopping board. Slice
beef thinly with a sharp knife.

Arrange salad leaves and slices of beef on a plate. Add onion slices and garnish with
pieces tomato. Drizzle dressing over the meat; serve with wasabi if desired.

Accompany with plum sake or sake.

This dish can be made using bonito or tuna instead of beef.

SASHIMI SALAD

serves 2

1 raw sashimi-quality snapper fillet
baby green salad leaves
1 tomato, sliced
1 spring onion, chopped
1 teaspoon capers

DRESSING
1 tablespoon rice vinegar
1 teaspoon caster sugar
1 tablespoon olive oil
1 tablespoon soy sauce

lemon wedges
1 stem common mint

Slice snapper fillet into sashimi
   Arrange green salad leaves and tomato on a plate.
   Place sashimi snapper slices in centre.
   Top with spring onion and capers.
   Make dressing by combining all ingredients in a bowl and sprinkle over salad and
sashimi.
   Serve with the lemon wedges and mint leaves placed off to the side.

This dish makes a nice accompaniment to both Japanese and western dishes.

Marinated salmon

Serves 2 as an entrée

A sashimi dish such as this may look quite exotic to a non-Japanese person, but it is really very simple and can be prepared very quickly at home and dressed down or up according to the occasion.

3 salmon sashimi slices (page 52)
¼ brown onion, thinly sliced and soaked in water

VINEGAR MIXTURE
½ cup rice vinegar
1 tablespoon caster sugar
a pinch of salt

6 small sticks of fresh ginger, cut as very fine julienne
1 stem common mint

Prepare salmon sashimi slices.
 Drain onion well.
 Combine all the ingredients for the vinegar mixture in a bowl.
 Marinate salmon slices with onion slices in vinegar mixture for 30 minutes.
 Transfer onion slices to a plate and top with salmon slices and criss-crossed ginger sticks. Arrange sprigs of mint on top of the ginger sticks.

Green shrimps (prawns) and salmon sashimi

Serves 4

As you are serving raw prawn flesh, it is important to use sashimi-quality prawns,

200 g (6½ oz) daikon radish
1 Lebanese cucumber
8 sashimi-quality green king prawns
400g (13 oz) sashimi-quality salmon fillet

Soy sauce for serving
⅓ cup wasabi paste or powder
4 lemon slices, to serve
4 sprigs shiso

Make a tsuma (garnish) using daikon. Traditionally it is prepared by peeling off in a continuous sheet and slicing. However, for the novice, use a vegetable peeler or Japanese-style slicer to slice off thin daikon strips. Roll up and cut into thin julienne. Then soak in water until used.

To make cucumber tsuma, slice off the skin and roll up, then cut into thin julienne. Soak in water until used.

To prepare the prawns, firstly remove the heads and set them aside. With belly side up, use scissors to cut away a strip of shell along the length of the prawn to allow you to lift out the body of the prawn with your finger, taking care not to break the shell.

Rinse the heads and shells, and cook in boiling water until they become red. Drain and cool down.

Drain daikon and cucumber tsuma well, and serve on individual trays.

To slice salmon, trim and cut salmon block to a 2.5cm by 5cm (1 x 2ins) rectangular block. Slice into 0.7cm (⅓ in) thick slices, cutting against the grain. Place on the daikon.

For the king prawns, put the flesh back into the shell and arrange on the cucumber with its head.

Serve with soy sauce and wasabi.

CALAMARI SASHIMI

2 teaspoons kuzu (starch)
1 cup (250 ml/8 fl oz) water
2 pieces cucumber peel, 20 cm (8 in) long
4 calamari, 150 g (5 oz) each, cleaned
4 thin strips salmon, 10 cm (4 in) long
4 lime wedges

DIPPING SAUCE
4 small leaf-shaped cucumber skins
4 small leaf-shaped carrot pieces
4 teaspoons powdered wasabi
2 tablespoons soy sauce

In a pan, combine the kuzu and water and bring to a simmer while whisking. Remove the pan from the heat just before it comes to the boil. Leave to cool at room temperature until the mixture is lukewarm.

In the meantime, make cucumber string by halving and slicing the cucumber peel thinly so that it resembles string. You will need 4 strips, each about 10 cm (4 in) long.

Prepare calamari following the steps on page 150. Place the cleaned calamari on a board, and with a filleting knife cut into very thin julienne strips, each about the thickness of a soba noodle.

Divide the calamari julienne into four and pack into a neat row on each serving plate. Top each with a salmon strip and a cucumber string (you can interlace them as in the picture if you like). Pour the kuzu over the calamari and garnish with fresh lime. Serve with the dipping sauce on the side.

To make the dipping sauce, use a small leaf-shaped cutter (or knife) and make four 'leaves' of cucumber skin. Make the four leaf-shaped carrot pieces in the same way, as well as four leaves of wasabi. You will find it easier to achieve the result if you use powdered wasabi mixed with a few drops of water, rather than wasabi from a tube.

Place a wasabi leaf on top of each carrot leaf, and top with a cucumber leaf. Carefully place each pile in the middle of a small dish of dipping sauce.

Alternatively, for a simpler accompaniment to the calamari, combine the juice of a lime with the soy sauce and wasabi to make a dipping sauce.

Stews

Stews and hot pots

Nabe is the Japanese word for pan or pot, so nabe-mono probably equates to the Western casserole, though the cooking methods may be different. Nabe-mono are usually cooked on a portable burner, or in an electric pot or frying pan at the table, with everyone sitting around, serving themselves from the pot, adding in extra ingredients and supervising the cooking. In some ways, it is rather like the European fondue style of cooking. It is a most pleasant way to warm up in winter. Soy sauce and dashi are the predominant flavourings, often with a touch of sweetness. It is a simple way of cooking. Meat or seafood and vegetables are cut up beforehand, and cooked in a dashi mixture which is simmering in a pot on the table. If a portable burner is not available, the meal can be cooked in a pot on a regular stove and brought to the table, which is just as tasty, but of course does not create quite the same cosy atmosphere.

Nabe are usually served with a side dish of steamed rice. Sake makes a good accompaniment, as does dry white wine.

BEEF AND VEGETABLE STEW

serves 2

1 new potato, cut into small pieces
vegetable oil
200 g (7oz) finely sliced brisket beef
or oyster blade (Finely sliced beef
is available from Asian butchers
or Japanese groceries.)
1 small onion, peeled and sliced
1 carrot, peeled and cut into pieces
½ packet shirataki noodles (gelatinous

noodles) or rice noodles
¼ cup caster sugar
2 tablespoons mirin
2 cups water
2 cups super dashi
4 tablespoons soy sauce
6 snow peas, trimmed
rice balls

Trim corners of potato to avoid breaking when cooking.

Pour a little oil in a saucepan and swirl over the base.

Add beef, onion, potato, carrot and shirataki noodles; stir for a couple of minutes.

Add sugar and mirin; stir again.

Pour water and dashi into the pot. Cook for 15 minutes, occasionally removing the scum from the surface.

Add soy sauce and snow peas and simmer with a lid on for a further 15 minutes.

Serve with rice balls or a bowl of steamed rice.

SUKIYAKI

Serves 4

600 g [1 lb 5 oz] Scotch fillet or sirloin fillet, finely sliced (slicing the fillet half-frozen makes it easier)
1 large packet momen (firm) tofu, cut into small cubes
1 carrot, cut in julienne slices
8 fresh or dried and soaked shiitake
1 bunch edible chrysanthemum leaves (available from Asian grocery stores)
4 spring onion stems, cut diagonally
¼ Chinese cabbage

1 packet harusame noodles or udon noodles cooked and drained
4 eggs
vegetable oil

SUKIYAKI SAUCE
⅓ cup caster sugar
3 tablespoons mirin
⅓ cup soy sauce
500g super dashi (page 66)
steamed rice, as accompaniment

There are regional differences in the preparation of sukiyaki. In the Tokyo area, sukiyaki sauce mixture (warishita) is made beforehand, whereas in the Osaka area, the sugar, mirin, soy sauce and dashi are added during cooking. Cooking is always done at the table.

Prepare meat, vegetables and noodles and place on a plate.

Break eggs into individual bowls and beat lightly.

Make sauce by combining all ingredients.

Set a portable cooking plate or electric frying pan on the table and heat.

Oil the pan, and start cooking by sautéing the spring onion, then add some of the beef, followed by small portions of the other ingredients and the sukiyaki sauce, a little at a time. Make a space for further ingredients by pushing the cooked ones to one side with chopsticks.

As the food cooks, guests can serve themselves by dipping the hot food into the beaten raw egg and eating with a bowl of rice.

When the pot has been cooking for some time, the taste will become quite concentrated.
At this stage, instead of adding sukiyaki sauce, water or a little sake can be added.
Other ingredients such as enoki or shimeji mushrooms can be included.

Shabu-shabu

Shabu-shabu is a word which cannot be translated directly, but it represents the sound made by the slices of meat as they are swished around the pot when dipped in the stock, rather like the lapping of water on the side of a boat.

Traditionally, this dish would be served at home with a side dish of steamed rice.

500 g (1 lb 2 oz) thinly sliced sirloin beef (available frozen from Asian butchers or Japanese groceries.)

500 ml (¾ pt) water

a sheet of kombu (dried kelp), approx. 5 x 10cm

¼ Chinese cabbage leaves cut into bite-sized pieces

1 packet enoki mushroom,stems dicarded

1 small packet silken tofu, cut into cubes

1 packet fresh shiitake (or 8 dried shiitake, soaked)

1 packet harusame noodles, cooked according to directions on packet

1 bunch edible chrysanthemum leaves (available from Asian and Japanese grocery shops)

1 x 5cm (1¾ in) length of peeled daikon, with red chilli inserted through slits, then grated

Soak kombu in water in a large saucepan or casserole dish.

Prepare the meat and vegetables and arrange on a large plate.

Heat water and kombu dashi in a pot on a portable cook top or electric frying pan on the table. Bring to the boil with lid on. When boiling, remove the kelp.

Family and guests sit around the pot and start cooking. Keep stock simmering continually. Using chopsticks, add beef, cooking until it just changes colour. Add vegetables to the pot, a little at a time.

Remove portions from the stock, dip into sauces and eat with daikon.

Seafood hot pot

Serves 4

1 litre kelp dashi
2 snapper fillets, cut into bite-sized pieces
a pinch of salt
4 scallops in shells
8 green king prawns
8 cockles
8 dried shiitake, soaked
1 bunch edible chrysanthemum leaves
¼ Chinese cabbage
1 packet harusame noodles or rice noodles, cooked and drained
1 cup goma-dare (white sesame seeds), vinegar-soy sauce (su-jyo–yu) or ponzu dipping
    sauce
½ cup grated daikon radish

Heat kelp dashi in a large casserole dish or saucepan.
   Place snapper in a bowl and rub with salt. Stand for 5 minutes.
   Prepare other ingredients and place on a large plate. Put dipping sauce into
individual bowls. Place daikon radish in a bowl. Set them on the table.
   Set portable stove or electric pan on the table.
   Put kelp dashi in the pot and simmer.
   Add some of the snapper fillets and other ingredients and simmer. Discard any scum
which may float to the surface.
   Diners can serve themselves, using chopsticks, and dipping food into the sauce. Add
more ingredients to the pot as the contents get low.
   Serve accompanied by dipping sauces and daikon.

Goma-dare dipping sauce

3 tablespoons sesame paste (or substitute tahini),
1 tablespoon sake
4 tablespoons caster sugar
1 teaspoon soy sauce
4 tablespoons roughly ground white sesame seeds

Combine sesame paste, sake and sugar in a bowl and stir until well mixed.
  Add soy sauce and sesame seeds and mix in well.

Ponzu dipping sauce

½ cup light soy sauce
½ cup lemon or lime juice
⅓ cup rice vinegar
1 tablespoon tamari soy sauce
3 tablespoons mirin
1x 5 cm kelp sheet, finely shredded

Combine all the ingredients. Allow sauce to stand overnight.

Vinegar-soy sauce

½ cup soy sauce
½ cup rice vinegar
1 teaspoon mirin

Combine all ingredients.

Homemade light-tasting soy sauce

1 cup soy sauce
2 cups super dashi
1 tablespoon sake
1 tablespoon mirin

Combine all ingredients.

Bring to boil, and simmer for 5 minutes. Store in a capped bottle in the refrigerator for 1 month.

Tofu

Tofu

Fresh or dried soy beans are delicious cooked in a variety of ways, but there are also many products in the Japanese diet derived from soy beans. The most common of these are soy sauce, tofu, nattou (fermented beans), soy powder and soy milk. The white bean curd known as tofu appears regularly on Japanese tables. Being a rich protein source, it is a healthy substitute for animal products. Depending on how much liquid is extracted from the curds during the manufacturing process, it becomes silken tofu (kinu-goshi-do–fu) which is quite soft and difficult to handle, or cotton tofu (momen-do–fu) which is much firmer. It is also available as deep fried tofu (abura-age) sold in block form or as pouches used in inari-zushi.

Vacuumed-packed fresh tofu is available from supermarkets everywhere. Once you've opened the packet, refrigerate any leftovers in water in an airtight container. Change the water every day and the tofu will remain fresh for a couple of days. If you detect a sour smell, discard it.

Before cooking tofu, it is best to extract the liquid from the tofu, unless you are cooking a hot pot. To do this cover over with a piece of muslin cloth or kitchen paper. Remove tofu from packaging and place on the cloth. Fold the edges of cloth over the tofu to wrap it. Press with a weight and stand for 20 minutes or so. In humid or hot weather, refrigerate.

It is often eaten on its own with a dipping sauce or in a miriad of dishes such as miso soup, miso dengaku (grilled tofu), sukiyaki and mizutaki (seafood hot pot).

Hot pot tofu

DIPPING SAUCE
4 tablespoons soy sauce
2 tablespoons rice vinegar
2 tablespoons mirin
1 piece dried kelp, cleaned
1 litre water
1 large, approx. 500 g (1 lb 2 oz)
packet of silken tofu, cut into
about 4 cm (1¾ in) cubes
shichimi (Japanese seven-spice)

CONDIMENTS
1 tablespoon daikon radish
with chilli, grated
1 tablespoon grated fresh ginger
1 spring onion, chopped

Combine dipping sauce ingredients in a saucepan and bring to the boil. Cool and pour into individual dipping bowls.

In a large heatproof pot, soak kelp for at least 15 minutes, then bring to the boil.

Place tofu onto the kelp, cover and bring back to the boil. Add Japanese seven-spice to taste. Serve in the pot with the condiments sprinkled on top and the dipping sauce on the side.

To make daikon with chilli, use a chopstick to make several holes on the cut side of daikon.
Insert a whole fresh red chilli into each hole and grate along the cut edge of the daikon to
make an attractive red and white garnish.

Chilled tofu with topping (traditional-style)

Serves 1

⅙ small packet silken tofu
1 teaspoon fresh grated ginger
¼ spring onion, chopped
a pinch bonito flakes
soy sauce for serving

Place cut tofu onto a plate, top with ginger, spring onion and bonito flakes.
   Serve with soy sauce.

Chilled tofu with topping (modern-style)

serves 2 as an entrée

1 tablespoon extra virgin olive oil
1 anchovy, chopped
¼ garlic clove, chopped
1 cherry tomato, rinsed and chopped
1 teaspoon lemon juice
1 teaspoon soy sauce
2 small green salad leaves
⅙ small packet silken tofu

Place a non-stick frying pan over a high heat and add a little olive oil. Add anchovy and garlic and stir over moderate heat for 2 minutes. Transfer to a bowl.
   Add tomato and pour in lemon juice and soy sauce while mixing.
   Place green salad leaves and tofu in a bowl.
   Top with anchovy and tomato mixture.

WHITE TOFU SALAD

Serves 2 as an entrée

¼ small packet of silken tofu
a pinch of roasted white sesame
seeds, ground
½ teaspoon caster sugar
⅓ tablespoon light colour soy sauce
1 tablespoon raisins, soaked in water
1 sprig common mint

Place a thick sheet of kitchen paper and tofu on a rack on a plate. Put a weight on top and stand for 15–20 minutes. Pat tofu dry with kitchen paper and place into a bowl.

Grind sesame seeds in a mortar and pestle.

Add tofu and mix in well.

Stir in sugar and soy sauce.

Add raisins and mix through.

Serve in a bowl, with mint as a garnish.

Ripe persimmon, pear or mango can be substituted for raisins.

Deep-fried tofu

Serves 2

⅓ small packet of silken tofu

SAUCE
½ cup super dashi
2 tablespoons soy sauce
1 tablespoon mirin
1 tablespoon grated daikon radish
potato starch for coating
vegetable oil
½ stem of spring onion, cut lengthways
into thin strands

Press and drain tofu for 15-20 minutes. Cut into two squares, approx. 5 cm. Pat tofu dry with kitchen paper.

Meanwhile, prepare sauce by simmering dashi, soy sauce and mirin in a saucepan for 3 minutes.

Squeeze grated daikon lightly with hands to remove liquid and set aside.

Dip tofu in potato starch and coat on all sides.

Place oil in a tempura pan or heavy frying pan and heat to 170°C (340°F) over a high heat.

Carefully slide tofu into the oil and deep-fry over a medium heat until the surface becomes crispy and golden brown. Drain on a rack or kitchen paper.

Pour sauce into bowls, and add tofu. Top with grated daikon and spring onion.

Miso soup

There are many varieties of miso available in Japan, but outside Japan the most frequently found varieties are red miso, brown miso and white miso. Brown miso has a well-balanced flavour and aroma; red miso has a stronger flavour; white miso is sweeter and less salty.

Miso soup is served in homes, restaurants and cafeterias daily throughout Japan. It is a valuable source of protein in the Japanese diet.

4 cups super dashi
2 tablespoons light brown miso paste,
mixed well with 1 tablespoon mirin
¼ small packet silken tofu, cubed
1 pinch of dried wakame-seaweed,
soaked in water
1 spring onion stem, chopped

Bring super dashi to boil in a saucepan.
Add miso and dissolve over low heat.
Add tofu and wakame and simmer for a couple of minutes.
Pour the soup into individual bowls.
Sprinkle spring onion over the top.

Other ingredients such as sliced abura-age (deep fried tofu), pumpkin, potato, carrot, beans, shiitake mushrooms or zucchini can be added.

Deep frying

Deep-frying

Deep-frying was introduced to Japan from Europe and China in 16th century. Since then, the method and ingredients have been adapted to meet Japanese ways, finally developing into tempura as we know it today. In a strange turn of events, tempura now travels back to the world it came from, and beyond.

The styles of deep-frying at home are divided into three categories: kara-age, lightly coated with flour or potato flour, tempura, coated with tempura flour and furai, coated with breadcrumbs.

Deep-fried eggplant

Serves 2

1 tablespoon mayonnaise
½ teaspoon wasabi paste
1 tablespoon mayonnaise, extra
1 teaspoon light brown miso
3 baby eggplants
3 tablespoons potato starch for coating
vegetable oil for deep-frying

To make wasabi mayonnaise, mix mayonnaise and wasabi in a bowl.
To make miso mayonnaise, mix mayonnaise with miso paste in a bowl.
Cut bottoms off eggplants so they will stand up. With a vegetable peeler, shave off the top layer of skin in stripes down the length of the eggplants. With a sharp knife make several incisions through the thickness of the eggplant to allow for more even cooking.
Coat with potato starch, patting in with hands.
Heat up oil in a heavy pan to approx. 170°C (340°F).
Deep-fry eggplants until the skin colour changes to bright purple.
Drain on a rack or kitchen paper.
Serve with mayonnaise.

TEMPURA WITH KING PRAWNS AND VEGETABLES

Serves 1

TEMPURA BATTER
1 cup tempura mix flour
1 cup cold water
3 green king prawns, deveined
5 carrot sticks
1 slice pumpkin
1 shiso (Japanese basil) leaf
1 seasoned small nori sheet (6 cm x 2 cm)
vegetable oil for deep frying

1 tablespoon sesame oil
potato starch or extra tempura flour for
    coating

DIPPING SAUCE
½ cup super dashi
1 tablespoon soy sauce
1 tablespoon grated daikon
½ teaspoon grated ginger

To make tempura batter mix, place flour in a bowl. Add refrigerated cold water. Using a pair of chopsticks or fork gently combine.

To prepare prawns, remove the head and shell without cutting off the tail. With a small knife, make a slice from the belly side to open like a butterfly.

Prepare oil in a deep pan and heat to about 180°C (350°F).

Coat prawns and vegetables with potato starch.

To check the temperature, drop a small amount of the tempura batter into the oil, and when it quickly floats up, it is ready. Holding one ingredient with tongs, carefully slide it into the oil.

Turn over when it becomes light golden colour, and remove when cooked on both sides.

Drain on paper towel.

Repeat with other ingredients. With thin ingredients like nori or shiso leaves, fry quickly.

Serve with tempura dipping sauce (made by mixing ingredients together) and a side dish of grated daikon topped with ginger.

Tempura is best eaten just after cooking, so when you are making tempura, have the rest of the meal ready and the table set so that tempura is the last thing you cook before eating.

Tempura can be eaten as a dish on its own, with rice, in dishes such as tendon

If you are unable to obtain tempura flour, make a batter using 1 cup plain flour, 1 beaten egg and 1 cup cold water.

Always coat tempura ingredients in potato starch before dipping into the batter.

Deep-fried skewered beef and vegetables

3 skewers

6 cubes lean rump beef
3 small fresh green chillies, seeded, or
    green capsicum, cut into bite-sized
    pieces
½ small onion, cut into 3
    (do not separate layers)
3 quail eggs
1 cup plain flour
1 egg, beaten
3 cups dry breadcrumbs (Japanese
    breadcrumbs, if available, are slightly
    coarser than Western ones.)

DIPPING SAUCE
English mustard
tonkatsu sauce, available in Japanese or
    Asian grocery shops

SAVOURY MAYONNAISE
1 boiled egg, mashed
1 pickled gherkin, finely chopped
parsley, chopped
1 tablespoon mayonnaise
lemon wedges
bamboo skewers

Skewer first 4 ingredients onto bamboo sticks.

Coat the skewers with flour and dip into beaten egg. Place into the breadcrumbs and coat evenly.

Heat up the oil as for tempura (page 142).

Deep fry until golden brown and drain on kitchen paper.

Serve with dipping sauce, savoury mayonnaise and lemon wedges.

To make savoury mayonnaise, combine boiled egg, gherkin and parsley with mayonnaise.

Optional ingredients include oysters, cheese (such as camembert or brie), asparagus, fresh shiitake, eggplant, onion, pumpkin or garlic.

Japanese-style pork cutlet

Serves 4

4 pieces pork loin (approx. 150 g [9 oz])
a pinch of salt
a pinch of cracked black pepper
1 cup flour
2 eggs, beaten
3 cups coarse breadcrumbs

6 cabbage leaves, sliced and soaked in
  water
4 baby tomatoes, sliced
snow pea sprouts
tonkatsu sauce for serving, available from
  Japanese grocery shops

Salt and pepper the pork. Along the fat, make a few slits with a knife to prevent pork shrinking when deep-frying.

Coat pork with flour.

Beat the eggs in a bowl and dip in the pork.

Remove from the egg and place onto the breadcrumbs.

Coat pork evenly with the breadcrumbs, pressing firmly with the hand.

Heat the oil to 180°C (350°F).

Deep fry pork until golden brown. Drain well.

Place some sliced cabbage, tomato slices and snow peas on a plate.

Serve with tonkatsu-sauce.

Since most Japanese food is eaten with chopsticks, when serving larger cuts of meat such as pork loin, slice into bite-sized pieces before serving.

SAVOURY DEEP-FRIED CHICKEN

Serves 2

200 g (7 oz) chicken thighs,
cut into cubes

MARINADE
2 tablespoons soy sauce
1 tablespoon honey or caster sugar
1 teaspoon crushed garlic
1 teaspoon grated fresh ginger
2 tablespoons potato starch
vegetable oil for deep-frying

Marinate chicken cubes in the soy sauce, honey, crushed garlic and ginger and put in refrigerator for at least 30 minutes.

Remove chicken from the marinade; drain and coat with potato starch.

Heat up the oil to about 180°C (350°F).

Deep fry chicken cubes for 1 minute, take out and set aside for 1 minute on a tray.

Deep-fry chicken again for two minutes.

Drain well on kitchen paper.

This tasty chicken is just as good served cold, and is perfect for lunch boxes or a picnic.

Japanese croquettes

There are many varieties of Japanese croquettes, such as crab meat, curry and cheese. They are delicious served cold on sandwiches.

5 new potatoes, peeled	2 eggs
1 brown onion, peeled and minced	2 cups flour
vegetable oil	4 cups breadcrumbs
200 g (7 oz) minced beef	garden salad
1 teaspoon salt	tonkatsu sauce for serving, available from
a pinch of cracked black pepper	Japanese grocery shops

Cook potato until soft and drain.

Meanwhile, fry onion in small amount of oil until golden brown, stirring continuously. Add minced beef while stirring and season with salt and pepper. Stir until cooked through.

Mash potato with a potato masher in a bowl. Add onion and beef, and combine well.

Take about two tablespoons of this mixture in the palm of your hand and make a ball. Flatten and make into little oval shapes. (They can be left as round balls if you prefer, but oval shapes are traditional.)

Beat eggs in a bowl and place flour and breadcrumbs on separate plates.

With hands, pat flour around croquettes.

Dip into the egg and coat with flour; dip into egg again and then into breadcrumbs.

Repeat with all croquettes.

Heat up the oil in a heavy pan.

Deep fry croquettes. When they are golden brown on the outside, remove from the oil and drain well.

Serve with salad and tonkatsu sauce.

Teppanyaki
Japanese-style barbecue

Teppanyaki—Japanese-style barbecue

Teppanyaki is an informal method of cooking food on a portable cook-top or hotplate at the table. 'Teppan' literally means a metal plate or hotplate, and 'yaki' means to grill, roast or barbecue, so the word refers only to the style of cooking, and not the ingredients. There are myriad recipes, and you can use an electric frying pan or an outside barbecue as well. Such dishes as gyoza, okonomi-yaki, yaki-soba, grilled o-nigiri can be cooked on a hotplate too. Teppanyaki is enjoyable with alcoholic drinks such as sake, beer or white wine.

Unlike the dramatic performance of the Teppanyaki restaurants, the preparation, cooking and eating of teppanyaki at home is an easy and simple procedure. It is good for small parties, either indoors or outdoors, and suitable ingredients include bite-size pieces of chicken, beef, pork, liver, quail eggs, spring onions, mushrooms, small green peppers and so forth, which can be cooked singly or threaded onto skewers.

Teriyaki salmon

Teriyaki sauce is available from Japanese or Asian groceries or major supermarkets, but you can make your own.

TERIYAKI SAUCE
1 cup super dashi
½ cup soy sauce
2 tablespoons caster sugar
1 tablespoon mirin
1 tablespoon fresh ginger juice
(made by grating fresh ginger and squeezing over a bowl)
1 tablespoon sake
vegetable oil
2 small salmon pieces
a few green salad leaves

To make teriyaki sauce, add all the ingredients in a saucepan and bring quickly to the boil, reduce heat and simmer for 15 minutes.

Drop a little oil onto the base of the frying pan and swirl to coat.

Place salmon in the pan, fry over moderate heat for one minute each side. Add teriyaki sauce and cook 5 minutes over a low heat.

Serve in individual dishes, garnished with salad leaves.

Instead of salmon, tuna, beef or chicken can be used.
Try marinating ingredients in teriyaki sauce before wrapping with foil and cooking on the barbecue.

Pork with ginger soy sauce

Serves 2

1 cup teriyaki sauce
200 g (7 oz) sliced lean pork
1 teaspoon ginger juice (made by grating fresh ginger and squeezing over a bowl)

vegetable oil

1 garlic glove, crushed

½ brown onion, sliced

and soaked in water

2 cabbage leaves, sliced and

soaked in water

Prepare teriyaki sauce. Marinate pork in teriyaki sauce and ginger juice for 30 minutes.

Pour a little oil in the non-stick frying pan and stir-fry onion and pork for 5 minutes or until cooked.

Add sauce and cook another minute and serve with sliced cabbage on a plate.

SALT-GRILLED SHELLFISH

Serves 2

1 tablespoon sake (or mirin)
2 green king prawns (push a bamboo skewer through each prawn lengthwise to
    straighten it prior to grilling)
2 fresh oysters
2 cockles
1 tablespoon salt
2 tablespoons grated daikon
ponzu dipping sauce
2 lemon wedges
1 tablespoon chopped chives

Sprinkle sake over the shellfish.
    Sprinkle salt on top.
    Over medium heat, grill both sides of seafood.
    Serve with grated daikon, ponzu dipping sauce and lemon wedges.
    Garnish with chopped chives.

Small fish such as yellow tail or whiting can be used instead of the shellfish

Barbecued chicken

Yakitori is skewered chicken, flavoured with sauce or salt and grilled over a charcoal fire. In specialised small shops throughout Japan known as Yakitori-ya, barbecued titbits of chicken meat, livers, hearts, intestines and skin are served with alcohol. Yakitori-ya are always crowded with people on their way home after work.

1 cup teriyaki sauce
200 g (7oz) chicken thigh fillets cut into bite-sized cubes
8 chicken livers
8 chicken giblets
3 spring onion stems, cut into 3 cm (1¼ in) lengths
8 Japanese green peppers (or any colour capsicum), seeded and cut into bite-sized pieces
bamboo skewers

Make teriyaki sauce.
   Thread chicken ingredients, peppers and spring onion onto bamboo skewers.
   Cook skewers in a frying pan, grill under the griller, or barbecue on the open grill or hibachi (Japanese griller), turning often and occasionally brushing with sauce.

Dumplings gyo-za

Makes 10

DIPPING SAUCE
½ cup soy sauce cup
⅓ cup rice vinegar
1 teaspoon sesame oil
1 teaspoon chilli oil

DUMPLING MIXTURE
60 g (2½ oz) minced pork or king prawn
¼ teaspoon chopped garlic

1 teaspoon grated ginger
1 Chinese cabbage leaf, chopped
5 stems Chinese garlic chives (nira), chopped
a pinch of salt
10 round gyo-za or gow gee wrappers
vegetable oil
¼ cup water

To prepare dipping sauce, mix all the ingredients in a bowl.

Place all the dumpling fillings in a bowl and combine well.

Place a wrapper on a dry plate or board and, using one finger, wet round the edges.

Put 1 tablespoonful of filling on the centre of the wrapper.

Fold the wrapper over the filling, seal the edges together by pressing and making small pleats. Repeat with remaining wrappers.

Heat a non-stick frying pan and add a little oil, swirling around the pan.

Lay a few gyo-za side by side in one or two rows in the pan (depending on size of pan), and cook on one side until golden brown. Then using a spatula, turn over 1 row all at once (so as to avoid breaking the dumplings). Add water and put a lid on to steam. Steam for a couple of minutes or until most of the liquid has evaporated.

Serve hot with dipping sauce.

Gyo-za dipping sauce is available from Japanese grocery shops.

Savoury japanese pancake (okonomi-yaki)

Makes 1

OKONOMI-YAKI SAUCE
2 tablespoons Worcestershire sauce
2 tablespoons tomato sauce
1 tablespoon soy sauce
1 teaspoon caster sugar
50 g (2 oz) self raising flour
¼ cup milk
¼ cup super dashi
a pinch of salt

1 egg
1 spring onion stem, chopped
1 cup thinly chopped cabbage
2 king prawns or thinly sliced pork or
    cuttlefish
aonori (green-seaweed) flakes for topping
dried bonito flakes for topping
Japanese mayonnaise

To make okonomi-yaki sauce, mix ingredients together in a bowl.

Place flour, milk, super dashi and salt in a bowl and lightly stir.

Break an egg into the mixture and stir to combine.

Add spring onion and cabbage and mix.

Heat a non-stick frying pan over moderate heat, swirl oil over base of pan.

Drop the egg mixture into the pan. Top with king prawns.

Cook until bubbles appear on the surface. Turn over and cook for about 4–5 minutes occasionally flattening with a spatula, until cooked through.

Brush the top with okonomi-yaki sauce, and sprinkle aonori and bonito flakes on top.

Serve with Japanese mayonnaise.

Cheese and chicken can also be used in this dish instead of seafood or meat.
Okonomi-yaki sauce is also available from Japanese grocery shops.

Desserts

Desserts

Traditional Japanese desserts were not rich, often just fruit—persimmons, particularly dried persimmons, grapes, nashi pears and mandarins. Now there are many introduced fruits, but good-quality fruit can be quite expensive. In many households the mother cuts pieces of fruit and shares them out to the family after meals.

Most Western-style desserts are available in Japan and are usually served after a meal. They are also served with afternoon tea and many cafes specialise in this fashion. True Japanese desserts usually consist simply of beautifully presented fruit, but Japanese chefs are now creating 'cross-over' desserts—an enjoyable blend of both styles, with a typical Japanese twist.

Soy milk jelly with black sugar glaze

Serves 4

½ cup black sugar
¼ cup water
200 ml [⅓ pt] water
4 g agar agar powder (available
from Asian grocery shops)
2 tablespoons caster sugar
400 ml [⅔ pt] soy milk (without sugar)
4 cherries for garnish

To make black sugar sauce, place black sugar and ¼ cup water in a saucepan, and simmer for 3 minutes. Cool.

Place extra water and agar agar powder in a saucepan, and combine well.

Bring mixture to the boil, continuously stirring. Simmer for 2 minutes.

Add caster sugar and stir until dissolved.

Remove from the heat, add warmed soy milk and mix well.

Pour into a flat-based container and refrigerate until firm.

With cookie cutters, cut into star-shapes or simply slice. Serve on a plate, glazed with black sugar or decorated as you wish.

Cut into star shapes, this makes an attractive Christmas-season dessert. Japanese people love to celebrate festivals, and although Christmas is not a traditional festival, these days it is becoming embraced by the Japanese as another reason to party.

SOBA COOKIES

80 g (3 oz) soba wheat, ground,
available from health food shops
100 g (4 oz) plain flour
1 teaspoon baking powder
1 egg
80 g (3 oz) caster sugar
extra flour

Preheat oven to 180°C (350°F).
Sieve together soba wheat, flour and baking powder.
   Beat egg in a bowl. Add sugar and whisk to combine well.
   Add flour mix and stir with a spatula.
   Transfer the mixture onto a sheet of baking paper, sprinkle with a little extra flour and knead lightly.
   Wrap in plastic wrap and refrigerate for 30 minutes.
   Roll out the dough between sheets of non-stick baking paper until 5 mm [¼ in] thick. Cut the dough into shapes using cookie cutters.
   Place on baking trays lined with non-stick baking paper. Bake for 13–15 minutes at 180°C (350°F) until lightly coloured.

Ginger sherbet

1 tablespoon grated ginger	2 egg whites
150 g (5 oz) caster sugar	1 teaspoon gin (or rum)
1 cup water	finely grated lime zest and mint for garnish

Place ginger, caster sugar and water into a saucepan over high heat. Stir until the sugar has dissolved, and simmer for 5 minutes. Remove from the heat and set aside to cool.

Put the egg whites into a bowl and beat with a whisk until soft peaks form. Add cooled ginger mixture and gin, then stir to combine.

Transfer to a container, cover and set in the freezer for approx. 4 hours.

Every 30 minutes, stir with a fork and return to the freezer.

Serve in glasses topped with finely grated lime zest and mint leaves.

Sake granita

½ cup water
1 cup sake
½ caster sugar

Place water, sake and caster sugar in a saucepan over high heat. Stir until the sugar has dissolved. Remove from the heat. Allow to cool.

Transfer the mixture into an ice cube tray. When frozen, put the ice cubes in a plastic bag, wrap with a towel and break up with cooking hammer into crystals.

Serve as for ginger sherbet.

GREEN TEA CAKE

Makes 1 loaf-shaped cake

3 teaspoons green tea leaves
40 g (1½ oz) plain flour
45 g (1½ oz) cornstarch
¼ teaspoon baking powder
3 eggs, separated
80 g (3 oz) caster sugar
a pinch of salt
icing sugar
mattcha (green tea) powder

Line a 10 cm x 20 cm loaf tin with non-stick baking paper.

Grind tea leaves finely using a mortar and pestle.

Sieve flour, cornstarch and baking powder together in a bowl. Set aside.

Place egg yolks and sugar in a bowl and beat with a whisk. Place the bowl over a saucepan of water approx. 70°C (160°F) and whisk until the mixture becomes creamy white. Remove from the water. Continue to whisk for 3 minutes or until cool.

Whisk egg whites and sugar in a bowl until soft peaks form.

Add ¼ egg white to the egg yolk mixture and combine with a spatula. Add sieved flour and combine.

Add remaining egg white and tea leaves and fold in without breaking the form of the white.

Transfer mixture into the loaf tin. Place in pre-heated oven (160-170°C [320-340°F]) and bake for 30-40 minutes.

When cooked, allow to cool and, using a small sieve, dust half the cake with icing sugar and half with the mattcha powder.

Warabi-mochi cake

Warabi-mochi is a traditional summer dessert. Originally it was made of wild bracken starch; however, these days it is made of the starch from sweet potatoes and tapioca.

150 g (5 oz) packet warabi-mochi powder
Water

KINAKO COATING
Mix 20 g (¾ oz) kinako (soybean powder) and 20 g (¾ oz) caster sugar or jyohakutou (Japanese style of sugar). This is basic. If you like spice, add cinnamon.

MATTCHA–KINAKO COATING
Mix 1 teaspoon mattcha (green tea powder), 20 g (¾ oz) sugar and 15 g (¾ oz) kinako.

Mix warabi-mochi powder with water in a pan, according to the packet instructions.
    Cook over a low heat until transparent, mixing continuously with a wooden spatula.
    Moisten a mould or other container with a little water and pour in warabi-mochi.
    Stand in a bowl of icy water to cool it down.
    Do not refrigerate or its colour will change to white.
    While it is cooling down, make the coating.
    When it's cool, take out and cut into pieces (the size you prefer).
    Coat with kinako or mattcha-kinako mixture to serve.

Warabi-mochi powder is available from Japanese grocery shops. Jyohakutou is the most common style of sugar in Japan.

JAPANESE PANCAKE WITH GREEN SOY BEANS AND RED BEAN JAM

Makes 8

JAM
100 g (3 oz) fresh or frozen eda-mame (green soy beans)
70 g (2½ oz) caster sugar
Salt, pinch

PANCAKE
80 g (3 oz) plain four
1 egg
70 g (2½ oz) sugar
1 tablespoon honey
⅓ tablespoon baking soda, mixed with a teaspoon water
40 ml (1½ fl oz) water
Vegetable oil
80 g (3 oz) sweet tsubu-an (red bean paste)

To make the zunda jam, cook eda-mame for 7–8 minutes if fresh; as per directions on the package for frozen; and drain. Remove the hull. Using a mortar and a pestle or food processor, grind, then add sugar and salt and mix well.

To make pancakes, sift the flour, then whisk in the egg and sugar.

Mix honey and baking powder together with a spatula. Then add to flour and combine well.

Gradually add water into the pancake mixture and mix well.

Cover with plastic wrap and set aside for 30 minutes.

Heat oil in a frying pan and make small pancakes of approximately 10cm (4ins) across. Sandwich together with jam.

CHERRY FLOWER ICE-CREAM

Makes 4–6 scoops

10 preserved sakura flower petals
150 ml (5 fl oz) cream
200 ml (8 fl oz) milk
2 tablespoons caster sugar
3 egg yolks
4 sakura flower petals for garnish

Whiz sakura flower, cream and milk in a blender, then bring to boil in a saucepan. Remove from heat.

In a bowl, whisk sugar and egg yolks together until pale.

Gradually pour the hot milk mixture into the bowl, stirring with a wooden spoon.

Make the mixture into custard by cooking over a double boiler to the ribbon stage, stirring continuously with a wooden spoon.

While still hot, strain the mixture into a bowl.

Place the bowl in an ice bath until cold and then churn mixture in an ice-cream machine.

Green tea ice-cream

Makes 4–6 scoops

150 ml (5 fl oz) cream
200 ml (6 fl oz) milk
3 egg yolks
¼ cup caster sugar
¼ cup green tea powder mixed with 1 teaspoon water

Make custard following the recipe for cherry flower ice-cream.
   After the straining stage, add green tea mixture and stir well.
   Cool in an ice bath until cold and churn in an ice-cream machine.

BLACK SESAME ICE-CREAM

Makes 4–6 scoops

150 ml (5 fl oz) cream
200 ml (6 fl oz) milk
3 egg yolks
¼ cup (60 ml/2 fl oz) caster sugar
2 tablespoons black sesame seeds, lightly roasted and ground

Make custard following the recipe for cherry flower ice-cream.
   After the straining stage, mix in black sesame seeds.
   Cool in an ice bath until cold and churn in an ice-cream machine.

Index

About the Author

Hideo Dekura was born in Tokyo and started his training in his family's two restaurants. Here he learnt the principles of sushi and kappou-ryori food preparation, cooking and presentation. At the same time he studied the philosophy of Chakaiseki (the cuisine of the tea ceremony), Teikanryu Shodo (calligraphy), Ikenobo-Ryûseiha (flower arrangement) and Hocho Shiki (the ceremony of the cooking knife) from Iemoto-Shishikura Soken-sensei under the authority of Shijyoshinryû.

In 2007, the Japanese government presented Hideo with an award for making a significant contribution to the promotion of Japanese food and cooking.

Hideo runs the Japanese cooking studio, Culinary Studio Dekura, works as a food consultant and is known as an expert in all aspects of Japanese cuisine.